How To Draw

FANTASY STYLE

How To Draw
FANTASY STYLE

Scott Altmann

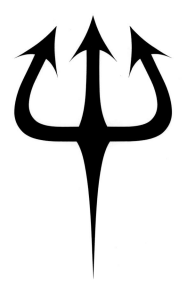

Search Press

This edition published in 2010 by
Search Press Ltd
Wellwood
North Farm Road
Tunbridge Wells
Kent TN2 3DR
www.searchpress.com

A Quintet book
Copyright © Quintet Publishing Limited
All rights reserved.
QTT.DHFA

This book was conceived, designed and produced by
Quintet Publishing Limited, The Old Brewery, 6 Blundell Street,
London N7 9BH, UK

Project Editor: *Martha Burley*
Assistant Editor: *Carly Beckerman-Boys*
Designer: *Rehabdesign*
Art Editor: *Zoë White*
Art Director: *Michael Charles*
Managing Editor: *Donna Gregory*
Publisher: *James Tavendale*

Printed in China by Midas Printing International Ltd.

Library of Congress Cataloging-in-Publication Data available upon request

ISBN: 978-1-84448-631-1
10 9 8 7 6 5 4 3 2 1

Contents

INTRODUCTION

The fantasy art genre is a broad one. However, there are popular themes and techniques which encompass the genre. This introduction supplies you with a suggested general toolkit, technical know-how and inspirational influences so that you can get started on fantastic utopias and dreamlike visions.

INTRODUCTION

**was in my Social Studies class, and it was my last
year of high school. Habitually, my notes and
writings began to morph into shapes, patterns,
designs and lines. Soon there was tone and form.
Once again I had begun to daydream and leave
my surroundings.**

The page took on a dark appearance, as grotesque monsters with
gnarled teeth and twisted mouths covered the entire page. Blood and
skulls were clumped together like some kind of horrid breakfast cereal
for a demon. My ballpoint felt as if it had been filled with some witch's
poison instead of ink. Suddenly, I heard the steps of my teacher walk up
behind me but I was too immersed in my own world to cover up my
actions. Any sudden moves would just further embarrass me,
so I simply froze and waited as I received my inevitable punishment.
She peered over my shoulder, and with a big smile said, 'Wow. That
is beautiful.'

After years of studying art and building my career I often think about
that moment. Surely my teacher could not have thought the scene I was
illustrating in Social Studies was particularly lovely or tranquil. It certainly
was not relevant to the subject we were all supposed to be focusing on.
I did draw better than my fellow students, but my skills were far from
being breathtaking. What made this vile drawing beautiful?

Today, I believe it was allowing someone else to view my imagination. The
ability to give an outsider a glimpse inside your own mind is very much a
beautiful thing. At its very fundamentals, this is the goal of fantasy art.

Left Fantasy art can twist reality and encourage it to take the form of something ethereal – from environments to creatures. **Above** The variety of projects in this book can form an introduction to fantasy art so that you can then explore your own options for creating wonderful characters and utopian visions.

Using this book

It takes considerable time and skill to be able to communicate one's imagination with paper or canvas. Perhaps you have wonderful worlds and characters in your dreams, but cannot transfer their image to paper? The aim of this book is to help you do this. Through several exercises ranging from drawing foundations to techniques used on a professional level, you will learn necessary skills to help you on your way to creating your own fantasy art.

TRADITIONAL TOOLKIT

I could fill an entire book with all the various tools and abundance of art supplies in my studio. Let us just cover the essentials, and review the items I use on a regular basis.

SKETCHING AND DRAWING SUPPLIES

- Sketchbook – various sizes
- Mechanical pencils – 0.5 mm 2B or HB lead
- Coloured pencils – various colours
- Kneaded eraser

PAPER

Bristol Vellum 68 lb (148 gsm), pictured left, provides a nice smooth paper, so that you can get fine detail. It still has a little bit of texture that I like. It can also take light watercolour/acrylic washes and ink well.

Rives BFK 140 lb (250 gsm) is intended for printmaking. This has a softer feel than other papers, and also a very natural texture. It is great for all media. Cold-pressed watercolour paper (140 lb/250 gsm) is a good paper if you desire a lot of texture, and a rougher, looser look. The rough texture makes it more difficult to render tight details. I also use this paper quite often to create textures that I will later scan and use in digital works (see the Texture Overlays in Photoshop box on page 80), and it can take pencils and paints equally well.

OIL PAINTING SUPPLIES

It is good to have a variety of bristle, sable and synthetic brushes. Flats, rounds, brights and filberts in various sizes are also needed. For detailed work I recommend Winsor & Newton Series 7 sable brushes. See pages 124–125 for an illustrated guide to the ideal oil painting kit.

PAINTS

- Titanium white
- Naples yellow light
- Cadmium yellow
- Cadmium orange
- Cadmium red medium
- Quinacridone red
- Transparent red oxide
- Alizarin crimson
- Raw umber
- Ivory black
- Viridian
- Cerulean blue
- Manganese blue deep

SURFACES

- Acrylic primed linen
- Masonite
- Illustration board

MEDIUMS

- Cold-pressed linseed oil
- Liquin
- Galkyd

PAINT SOLVENT

- Turpenoid

DIGITAL TOOLKIT

My approach to digital painting is fairly simple, and my set-up reflects that. Most of the tools you need are actually on the software you will be using.

MY COMPUTER

24-INCH MAC

A good monitor at a larger size is very beneficial to the visual artist. I find this important because this way you can work on larger portions of the painting without always having to zoom in. The constant zooming can be a problem, as you need to view the whole image in its entirety. Otherwise you will literally lose sight of the big picture.

4 GB RAM

It's always good to get as much RAM memory as you can afford. Developers are constantly upgrading their software, which usually means more RAM is required for the latest version. It will also help if you choose to run more than one painting application at once like I do.

BACK-UP DRIVE

The worst thing about computer crashes is that they usually come without warning and you never know when it is going to happen. Get a back-up drive, and make sure it backs up regularly. I have mine set to back-up my hard drive every hour. Countless hours of hard work could be lost if you do not take the proper precautions.

23 CM X 30 CM (A4 SIZE) TABLET

WACOM INTUOS 4

I prefer to use a larger tablet, but this is a personal preference. Some people find the additional space cumbersome and excessive. Perhaps it is because my background is in traditional painting, but it feels much more natural to me to have the larger tablet space. It is also good that I can draw and paint in longer and broader strokes, using arm movements more than just small hand and wrist movements.

SCANNER

EPSON PERFECTION 2400 PHOTO

This is an older scanner, yet still provides all the resolution needed. It has 2400 x 4800 optical resolution, but recent comparable models have at least twice that. I will scan drawings and small paintings in at anywhere from 300dpi to 600dpi.

PRINTER

EPSON STYLUS PRO R1800 INKJET PRINTER

My printer serves several purposes for me. It can accept paper up to 33 cm x 48 cm (roughly B3 size), which is good for prints. I also use a technique where I will print out a drawing and then mount the drawing onto a support. Once I prepare the surface, I can paint on top of that. The printer can serve many needs.

COREL PAINTER AND ADOBE PHOTOSHOP

In both applications I use extremely simple techniques. I will go over some very basic tools I use regularly.

PAINT BRUSH

For the bulk of my work I use a Round Brush with the Shape Dynamics set on Pressure. I also will use a Natural Media Brush for texture and for different edge control.

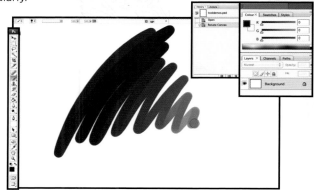

LASSO TOOL

This is great if you just want to work on a specific area while not affecting the rest of the painting. It is also very good for selecting certain elements and moving them around.

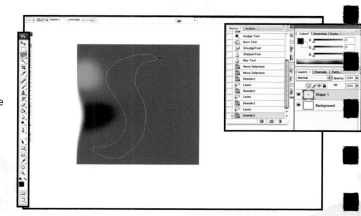

DODGE AND BURN

The Dodge and Burn tools can come in handy for lightening and darkening areas of your image.

DODGE

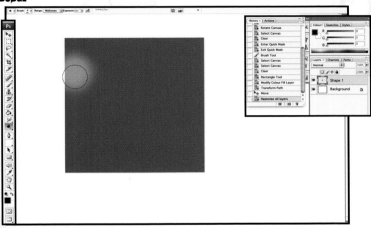

BURN

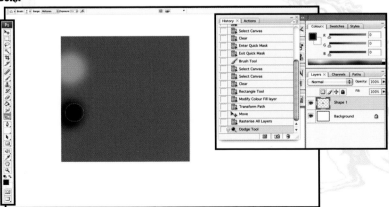

SMUDGE, BLUR AND SHARPEN

These are helpful both for edges and also for pushing elements back and bringing other elements forwards. They are also very good if you find an area needs more blending.

SMUDGE

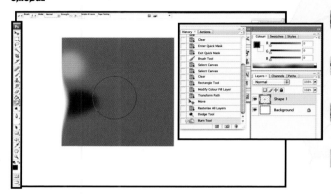

BLUR

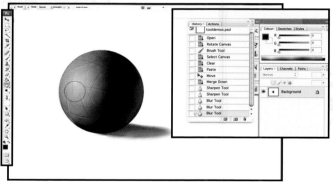

SHARPEN

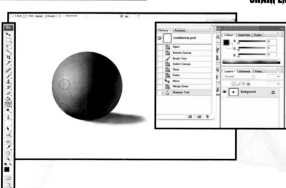

LAYER PALETTES

These are extremely useful when working both completely digitally but also when working on traditional media, and enhancing it digitally. The several layer options (Overlay, Multiply, Hard Light etc) give you endless options and possibilities.

ADJUSTMENTS

I like to make adjustments in the layer palette, since you can control how much it affects the entire piece. I mostly use the Levels Adjustment and Colour Balance options. Levels are used for controlling the light and dark values of your image. Colour Balance is good for fine-tuning colour. For information about adjusting levels, see page 119.

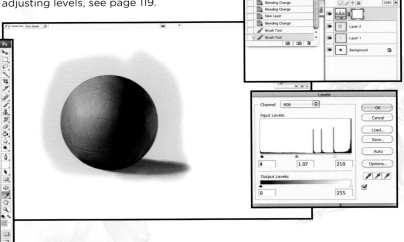

FANTASY STYLES

When we think of fantasy art many of us will picture dragons, spell-casting wizards and a heroic knight. The fantasy art genre is much more varied than that. Several styles and cross-genres now fall under the fantasy art banner.

The styles of fantasy are ever-expanding and frequently being combined with other genres to create something new – for instance, horror with fantasy might give you dark fantasy. The boundaries of fantasy style are non-existent, which is why it remains exciting and relevant today.

CLASSICAL OR TRADITIONAL

This is probably the most recognisable fantasy art. Picture damsels in distress, or dragons and knights on horseback. Often there will be roots in folklore. It is time-tested and still remains popular today.

CHILDREN'S AND YOUNG ADULT

Fairies, gnomes and trolls are quite common in these illustrations. Often you will see the hero or heroine portrayed as a child, so the viewer can identify themselves in the scenario.

MODERN

Not all fantasy takes place in
some primitive dark age. Magic
and supernatural occurrences in
a modern setting have helped keep
fantasy art current and remain an
important part of the genre's growth.

STEAMPUNK OR SCI-FI

Although many consider science
fiction an entirely different genre,
there is often a hybrid mix of the two.
With steampunk art, the style
incorporates a primitive technology,
yet with the ornamental and visual
aesthetic of fantasy art.

THE ROOTS OF FANTASY-STYLE

The roots of fantasy can be traced back to the earliest of religious paintings. Greek and Roman sculptures of their gods can all be considered early fantasy art. Now we consider them myths, but at the time they were trying to create art and imagery of things that they simply did not see. If you have seen an early painting depicting an angel, you already have seen the roots of fantasy art. Those artists' goals are not very different from our own. Perhaps the religious connotation is absent, but the goal of creating visuals that only exist in our imagination and sharing them with others is identical.

One only needs to open an art history book to see examples of the roots of fantasy everywhere. From Michelangelo's Sistine Chapel, to the Pre-Raphaelites of the mid 1800s, there are all the ingredients of fantasy art.

The Sistine Chapel

Ignoring the fact that Michelangelo was creating a religious-based artwork, the glorious Sistine Chapel is a real point of reference for the fantasy artist. The flayed skin of Saint Bartholomew is something right out of a horror-fantasy illustration, and the group of figures being sucked down into hell is another example of this. Look further up the ceiling, and we have several floating figures and angels that resemble paintings in current fantasy circles.

Above The Sistine Chapel, Apostolic Palace, Vatican City.

THE SYMBOLISTS

The artistic period that resembles the current state of fantasy art the most would be the Symbolist era, starting in the late 1800s and continuing through the 1900s. The term Symbolism is extremely broad, covering artists who worked in several styles and mediums, much like fantasy art does now. Artists like Gustav Klimt, John William Waterhouse and Edvard Munch, were all considered Symbolists. If they were alive today their work could be considered fantasy art.

Right Gustav Klimt, *Water Serpents*, 1904 (oil on canvas).

FANTASY INFLUENCE

Today, fantasy art has had a profound influence on our most popular entertainment mediums. Everything from children's fairy tales, to comic books, video games and film have all been influenced by the creative power of fantasy. The growing influence of fantasy art continues to expand, providing more directions for artists to share their imagination.

It is the job of the fantasy artist to help visualise these imaginary worlds and their inhabitants. Whenever you see a book cover that has a magic–wielding sorceress on it, or a video game with a horrific beast to fight off, a fantasy artist was likely to have been responsible for that creation. As technology improves in gaming and film, it opens the realms of what is possible, giving fantasy artists even more room to stretch their creative muscles.

Top Science fiction has always been seen to go hand-in-hand with fantasy art – from the glorious jacket designs to the monsters and worlds described within them.

Above The creation of computer-animated characters like Gollum has been influenced by fantasy art.

LOWBROW ART

Even the world of fine art has been influenced by the exciting possibilities of fantasy art. Many illustrators who have worked in the fantasy genre have crossed over and begun experimenting in the Lowbrow art, or the Pop Surrealist gallery scene.

The Lowbrow art movement is thought to have started in the 1970s. Artists, like Robert Williams, began adding humour and references to popular culture in their artwork. Usually the influence of comics and cartoons is apparent in the imagery. In some ways, it can be seen as a reactionary movement by artists to create something devoid of the pretentiousness of modern art, and provide art that was more universal. Lowbrow art can be interchangeable with the many subcategories that have been spawned, such as Pop Surrealism, Street art and Outsider art.

Left and above Works by Lowbrow Pop Surrealist artist Michael Forbes, 2005 (oil on canvas).

FANTASY STYLE NOW

Fantasy art has stood the test of time, and will continue to evolve and be a prominent genre in illustration. A big reason for this is the ability to incorporate topics and trends that are relevant at the current time. Fantasy art today is at one of the most exciting artistic stages in its progression. With the technological advantage of Internet communication and information, artists now have access to so much more than ever before. Artists from around the world are sharing ideas and learning from one another on a daily basis – something that was impossible not long ago.

KEEPING ART RELEVANT

The current climate of fantasy art is an exciting one, yet also highly demanding of the artists' technical and emotive abilities. The reason for this is directly related to the current trend in films and video games. With the rapid advances in technology in games and film, people are accustomed to seeing incredible imagery that pushes their imagination. It should be noted that artists were likely to have been responsible for that imagery in one way or another. So how will fantasy art be able to hold the attention of a fifteen-year-old boy who has just watched a film where flying aliens are jumping out of the screen in 3D? Or the child who just played a game where the monsters were so frightening they made him jump? Since fantasy art is 2D and static this task seems quite difficult.

This is one reason we are seeing such great fantasy art now. Not only do film and video games influence our art, it also pushes us to create stronger work. Character, creature and clothing designs have all been pushed further recently, resulting in imagery we haven't seen before. The worlds that are being created seem more vivid and tangible – giving us an endless playground for our imaginations.

Right Fantasy artists are continuously working hard to push boundaries and present new and exciting visual ideas.

STARS OF FANTASY ART

The list of masterful fantasy artists is ever growing. It would be impossible for me to list every one of the past and present. I urge you to not only seek out artists for yourselves, but to also go beyond the genre of fantasy art and look at what other art movements have to offer. The best fantasy art is usually a hybrid of multiple art movements. I spent most of my school years studying the traditional masters, such as Rembrandt and Vermeer, and later early twentieth-century artists like John Singer Sargent, J.W. Waterhouse and Alphonse Mucha to name a few.

There are many artists who are directly tied to the fantasy art movement who can influence you in learning the style.

ARTHUR RACKHAM (1867–1939)

Rackham worked in pen and ink, with muted watercolour. His work remains very popular even today. He painted great depictions of fairy tales, including *Alice in Wonderland*.

Above Arthur Rackham, *Up To the House-Top the Coursers They Flew*, illustration from *The Night Before Christmas* by Clement Clarke Moore, 1931.

WINSOR McCAY (1867–1934)

Winsor McCay worked in comic strips, but also later got involved as a pioneer in animation. I include him under fantasy art, for his famous *Little Nemo in Slumberland* comic strip. The dreamlike nature of the story resulted in some wonderful, surreal work.

FRANK FRAZETTA (1928–2010)

Frazetta probably has had one of the biggest impacts on modern fantasy illustration. He began in comics and later turned to painting. Known for unsurpassed anatomy in his figures and his Conan imagery, his work continues to have an influence on today's artists.

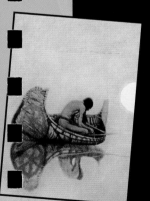

N.C. WYETH (1882–1945)

A student of Howard Pyle, Wyeth is known for his bold colour, brushwork and compositions. His paintings fall under a more classical form of fantasy art, as he illustrated *Robin Hood*, *King Arthur* and *Robinson Crusoe*. His son Andrew became an even more famous artist with work in major museums.

Top Winsor McCay, *Little Nemo in Slumberland*, from *The Denver Republican*, 1910.

Above N.C. Wyeth, *The Silent Fisherman,* published in *Scribner's Magazine*, 1907.

CHAPTER 1

IDEA CREATION

The formation of ideas, or ideation, is one of the most important parts of the creative process. All the greatest artistic rendering and technique cannot hide a weak concept. The flipside to that is that the best ideas will not communicate clearly unless the craftsmanship is equally great. Having a process to convey your ideas clearly is essential to creating great fantasy art.

IDEATION

Where will these ideas come from? The answer is everywhere and everything. It is your job as an artist to make sure you are inspired. A film, a riveting book, a trip to a museum, a nature walk – all are ways you can be inspired to create your next masterpiece. Inspiration and ideas will show up in strange and unexpected places. Always keep a sketchbook on you. Even a small pad will be sufficient to jot down ideas and rough sketches.

Lack of inspiration?

Most artists who claim they do not have any ideas are really suffering from a surplus of ideas. It can be overwhelming and a hard task to edit and sift through the many images in our head and pick the gems out of the rocks. Having a thought process will help you eliminate the weaker ideas before you invest too much time on them.

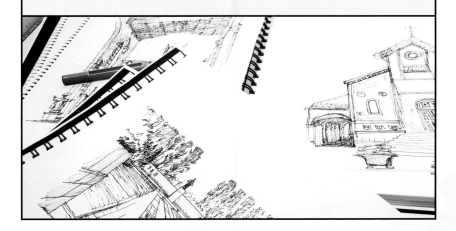

SKETCHING

Much of my approach to rough sketches depends on a few variables. Is it for a client? Is this a personal piece? Is this purely for fun and enjoyment?

Regardless of the end goal, I begin my rough sketches in a very loose and crude manner. Whether it is on my computer drawing digitally, or in my sketchbook, I work fast and without concern for how the sketch is looking. This is the beginning of a process – not the end result.

BEGINNING A SKETCH

Depending on how clear the visual is in your head, start abstractly with lines and sometimes tone. It could all be very random as it is a searching process. Pick out certain things that interest you or might take you another step closer to a developing idea. In a way, this very loose way of working requires more concentration and focus than painting an image that is already planned out. Your mind really has to be sharp to grab onto anything that is escaping from your subconscious and out through your fingertips.

THUMBNAILS

Thumbnails are great tools for any artist. They allow you to see if certain images will work or not before you take them to the next stage.

Keep to the **'three S'** rule to really maximise the benefits of thumbnails. I find I have to remind myself of this rule every now and then, so I do not get too involved with the thumbnail sketches.
- Small
- Simple
- Shapes

VALUE

Value in sketching means adding lightness and darkness into a sketch. When working with thumbnails, you need to focus on speed, so I try to minimise the amount of value I use to a maximum of three or four values. Most of the time I will only use two values if I am doing them very quickly. If the image is not reading at this stage, you either have to rethink it, or abandon it all together. To find out more about applying tones and values, see page 98.

BE CAUTIOUS

Thumbnails should only really be thought of as a beginning. There is still a significant amount of work to do once this stage is done. Rarely, you will find a thumbnail that seemed to work at a reduced size does not translate once enlarged. It is not a common occurrence, and one only need be aware of it in the early stages.

1. Thumbnails should show degrees and values of colour.
2. They can help you plan perspective and the angles in your work.
3. Avoid going into too much detail with your thumbnails. They should be simplistic in their approach.

REFERENCE IMAGES

The use of references is essential to creating representational fantasy art. You have to create a 'suspension of disbelief' by giving the viewer certain realistic elements to grab on to before you serve them the implausible. How realistic you want to be is up to you and will directly determine how you use your references.

Books and Internet searches are great for finding references. It is very important to be aware that you should in no way copy from photos that you did not take yourself. Aside from the strict copyright laws, as an artist you are doing yourself a disservice. Take the essential elements you need, but use your creativity and knowledge and apply it to your image.

TAKING YOUR OWN SHOTS

Most of the time you will want to take references for yourself. Your style will determine how involved your photo shoot will be. My work is fairly stylised, yet I do like a sense of realism, especially when it comes to lighting. A simple set-up of an inexpensive light and a camera set on a tripod may provide all the visual information you need. Use friends or pose yourself.

It is a good idea to take several photos with slight variations in pose and lighting. Take close-ups of hands and any other part you feel you may need detail for. You could convert your photos to black and white to clarify the values and also to force yourself to be more creative with colour.

Above Play with lighting and take several shots – the body may look better in one image but the posture in others.
Right The use of real props in your reference images can add realism to the final piece.

RESEARCH

In many cases, you will need to dig a little deeper than an Internet search to gain access to information not so easily accessible to you. Foreign locations, historical fashion and weaponry are all things that may require a bit more legwork. Libraries are still great resources for information and reference material. Even your local bookshop may have additional information that you just could not acquire from your computer.

Museums are another great place to do research. To see objects in direct observation is always preferable to a photo or an image on your monitor. It allows you to understand the intrinsic qualities of the object you are researching much more clearly. You are also more likely to gain the more subtle nuances and details of whatever it is you are researching.

Metropolitan Museum of Art

It is an understatement to say that the MMA in New York is a good place to see masterpieces of fine art. It is great for researching subject matter not normally considered art. There is probably no better place in New York City to get up close to weaponry and armour used throughout the centuries. The Costume Institute is an amazing resource to get inspiration for your fashion designs. Another

museum worth a visit is the Victoria and Albert Museum in London, which has a wide selection of historical artefacts and garments. Even your local museum is worth a visit for inspiration.

I find zoos are also perfect for researching animals. Much like the human figure, photos of animated animals tend to give them a frozen and wooden appearance. Observing an animal moving in real time and space can add additional energy and life to your work.

Take the time to do your research. It is very likely that the process of research will spark many new ideas along the way.

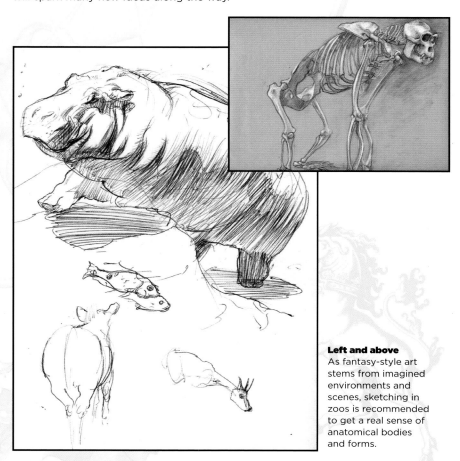

Left and above
As fantasy-style art stems from imagined environments and scenes, sketching in zoos is recommended to get a real sense of anatomical bodies and forms.

ALTERNATIVE METHODS

Having a process and method is extremely important for an artist, but occasionally there will be stumbling blocks. Perhaps your compositions feel weak or your character designs are uninspired. When that happens, there are a few things you can do that will help.

TAKE A BREAK

Walk away. Simply giving yourself that distance from a piece can be all you need to get reinvigorated and inspired again. Sometimes even letting a piece sit through the night is very helpful.

GO FOR IT

Sometimes all the preparatory work can drain the motivation and inspiration from you. Skip the rough sketch and thumbnail stages and begin drawing what you want as the focal point. Use it as an anchor for the piece, and let the image grow out from the focus. It is risky, but it can yield successful results.

ABSTRACTION

For some artists, this is very uncomfortable for them and only results in frustration. Other artists find this method very liberating, exciting and natural. Much of this depends on the individual. I find this method can yield unexpected yet highly energetic results. The process is simple and there is no right or wrong way to do it. Just begin with abstract shapes, tones and line using any medium, traditional or digital. Once you have an abstract image you find looks interesting, try to pull forms from that until you have the beginnings of an object that is representational. You might not get something right away, but be patient and try to go with the flow as much as you can.

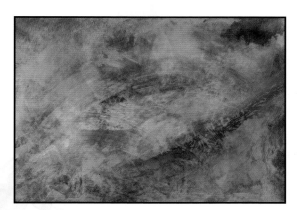

Left Abstraction technique begins with abstracted forms and colours, working on textures and tones that you feel create an atmosphere.

Above Working on top of the initial abstraction, you may find that you can experiment with overlapping forms and a naturalistic scene emerges.

CHAPTER 2

FANTASY CHARACTERS

Since the days of cavemen, humans have been drawing each other. Our art has become more sophisticated, yet we still latch onto characters. It helps us sympathise with and relate to what we are looking at. We can also see a character in an image and it will conjure feelings of anger or fear. In fantasy art, we do not have the luxury of following a character's journey. We are communicating through visuals, so the character design must read clearly.

CREATING CHARACTERS

Just as a jazz musician must know the scales to improvise, a fantasy artist must learn the visual language necessary to communicate his or her idea. Artists are fortunate, since we already have several psychological devices that can trigger the emotions and ideas we want. Angular and sharp shapes can evoke evil, while soft curves are often friendlier. Warm, bright colours are inviting and peaceful, while cool, muted colours can seem eerie and sombre. These are all conventions that you can break and experiment with, but make sure you are aware of them to begin with.

PREPARATION FOR IDEAS

Before you even make your first pencil mark, try to establish some basic ideas that you want to convey. Good or evil? We often associate black and darker colours with evil, and white and lighter colours can represent nobility. If you were to paint a white angel all black, it would appear as some wicked demon. That is a huge change just by using colour. Shape and size can also determine how we view a character.

Left Deciding on a colour scheme and choice of palette can help you get a feeling for the character – will they be bright and cheerful or dark and sinister, for example?

The impact of eyes

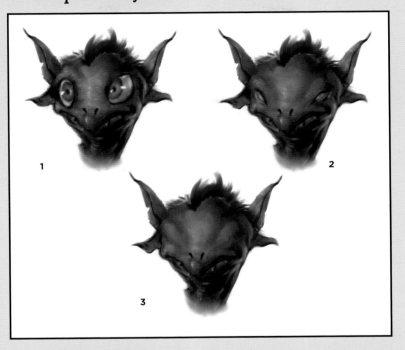

1

2

3

1. Big, round eyes on a little creature will make it seem cute and lovable.

2. Now replace those big, round eyes with tiny, angular eyes and the creature will appear sinister and mischievous.

3. Remove the eyes altogether and the creature will appear soulless and frightening.

SYMBOLIC INTERPRETATION

In some cases when creating
characters, you may want to think in
terms of symbols and shapes instead
of features and anatomy. Starting
with simple geometric shapes can
have a strong effect subconsciously,
as we tend to respond well to simple
shapes. Mickey Mouse, for example, is
made up of circles, and so appears
friendly and non-threatening. In
Pixar's movie *UP*, the main character,
Carl Fredricksen, is an old grumpy
man, and represented by a square-ish
head and body. This gives him a
slightly prickly, angular appearance.
The pointed hats of wizards and
witches are a triangular shape.
Triangles have been used to
represent divinity in history, but can
also represent power, which witches
and wizards certainly have.

Animation

I would recommend studying animation to get more ideas on how to
push your character designs. Often physical traits are extremely
exaggerated in animation, so it makes it easy for viewers to identify
and pick up on the make-up of the character.

TRIANGLE

I used an upside-down triangle for this man. Without seeing much, we start to get the impression that this man would be high ranking, powerful and unlikely to be a very approachable person.

BODILY PROPORTIONS

Proportions are the cause of many beginner artists' frustration and anxiety, but most of that is caused by over-thinking and misguided focus. The truth is we all know proportions much better than we think. If you see an image where the head is too big, you identify it immediately. Identifying similar problems in our own work merely requires stepping back and giving the picture an honest evaluation.

That does not mean you should dismiss some basic principles. If you ever need to check something, or need a base of comparison, it will serve you well.

THE FAIL-SAFE RULE

Using the head as a unit of measurement, the average human's proportions are seven heads in height. This measurement only works if the human is standing upright and is being viewed at eye-level. Any variation in pose such as crouching or sitting will not follow this proportion rule. A tilt in angle or perspective can also cause foreshortening and stray from this principle.

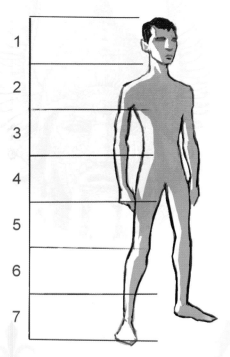

PLAYING WITH PROPORTIONS

Another common proportion scale is often called the 'ideal proportions'. Instead of a figure being seven heads high, it will be eight. The height does not need to change – only the head size in relation to the rest of the body.

If you want to create a character that is not average in appearance you will need to step outside the standard proportion guidelines. Perhaps you want to draw a character with massive musculature or one that is very thin? Keep in mind a hierarchy of design and proportion. Most likely if a character is very top heavy, the legs will need to be thick too so the character appears balanced. If a character is very thin, it will appear so, in everything from his limbs to his face. Of course, you may want to push these norms as well according to your style and ideas.

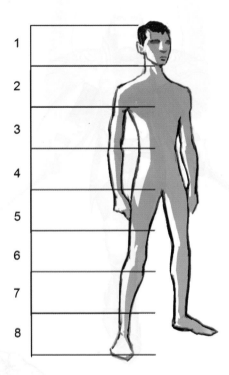

THE HUMAN HEAD

There have been countless studies, books and even documentaries focusing on the human head and face. It is how we identify each other, and it is most likely the first thing we look at when seeing a new person. Understanding the form and structure of the human head is important to creating solid, interesting characters and enhancing the level of your fantasy art.

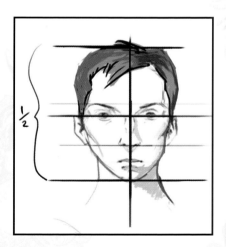

SIMPLIFY

The human head is quite complex, and therefore it is very beneficial to learn how to simplify it. If we were to simplify the head into a very basic shape, it would be a sphere with an axis down the middle. When drawing a head, start with an ovular shape, and depending on where the face is turned in space, locate the axis of the head and mark it. Then make a mark for the placement of the main features of the face – eyes, nose and mouth.

THE SKULL

It is very beneficial to study the human skull. It will give you a valuable understanding of the underlying structure of the head. Start with simple large shapes and as you progress refine the accuracy and smaller forms of the head.

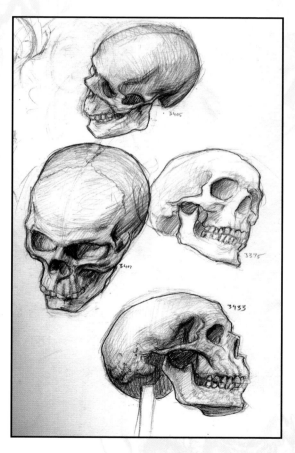

Left Studying the human skull can help you discover surprising facts about the proportions of the face – for instance that the eyes should actually be correctly positioned halfway down the head to give a sense of realism.

DRAWING THE HEAD

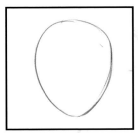

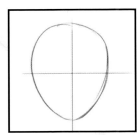

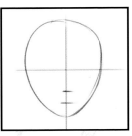

Step 1: I like to start with a simple oval, or an upside-down egg shape. It gives a good starting point for the natural taper of the human skull, as well as implying the roundness of the top portion.

Step 2: Find the centre and draw a line down the middle vertically. Halfway down draw a horizontal line to indicate where the eyes will be. It may seem far down, but the hairline covers a good portion of the top of the head.

Step 3: About halfway between the eye-line and the bottom of the chin indicate a line for where the nose will go. With that line established, draw a line halfway between the nose-line and the bottom of the chin to indicate the mouth placement.

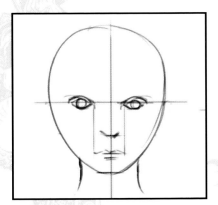

Step 4: Now begin drawing the eyes along the eye-line. Imagine that the line would be going halfway through the eyeball. The space between the eyes should be the length of one eye. To indicate the width of the lips, find the corners of the eyes, and draw vertical lines down to the previously placed mouth-line.

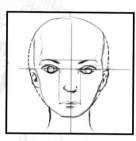 

Step 5: Approximately ²/₃ of the way between the eye-line and the top of the head you can place the eyebrows. At this point, you will want to refine the shape of the head, since our skulls are not shaped exactly like eggs. Indicate cheekbones, the overall shape of the forehead and the jawline. The top of the ears should line up with the eye-line.

Step 6: Refine. At this point you have established the general placement of the features and the proportions. Unless your figure is bald, you will want to add some hair. At this stage it is simply tweaking and adding the desired amount of detail.

Right Once the basics are in place the gentle contours of the face can be added using shading. White can help bring out highlights of the face.

TYPICAL FANTASY STYLE

Before we can begin to work outside the norms of fantasy art, it is a good idea to understand what makes up the typical fantasy style.

Above A typical scene – otherworldy and overwhelming.

SET THE SCENE

Primarily, we should establish the setting, which is parallel to the Dark Ages or medieval era. The should be very primitive technology by today's standards – weaponry should consist of mainly swords, shields, axes, bows and similar items. The heroes go to face their rivals on horseback, as opposed to facing them in a military tank. Armour and fashion are also based on a Dark Age, medieval time but there is flexibility to push designs a bit. Much of the ornamentation draws influences from Celtic designs and patterns. You will not be seeing blue jeans or hooded sweatshirts in typical fantasy-style art.

BE MORALISTIC

It is common to depict a clear good versus evil situation in a typical fantasy image. Our noble heroes represent the good, and the evil characters can sometimes be human but can also take on other forms. The use of magic and sorcery is a very common element in typical fantasy and can provide some wonderful, exciting imagery.

CREATURES FROM THE DEPTHS...

Aside from humans, it is important to recognise the other inhabitants in a typical fantasy setting. Most of these creatures have roots in folklore and fairy tales. Some of them include dragons, trolls, gnomes, goblins, fawns, centaurs, satyrs and fairies. The world in which they live is again parallel to the Middle Ages on Earth, with lush forests and castles for the kings and queens.

Many of these creatures share common traits that are repeated in different fantasy stories. Trolls, for example, are often depicted as ugly creatures with very long noses that are covered in warts. It is not unusual for a troll to have more than one head. The bodies of trolls are frequently described as misshapen or humpbacked regardless of their size.

Gnomes, unlike trolls, are fairly consistent in their small stature, averaging around a metre in height. Gnomes are frequently portrayed as having ample facial hair, which is often light in colour or grey. Their ears are similar to those of a human, but are lengthened to a point.

The overall physicality of fairies is very similar to humans. In fantasy literature, fairies are depicted as being tiny human beings with wings. As creatures that live in the forest, their clothing is fashioned from leaves, flowers, moss and vines.

Right Humans could take on traits from animals – for instance the wide shoulders, confident stance and wild eyes of this character seem almost gorilla-like.

VARIANTS

Take a sketchpad onto a train or bus, to a shopping centre or any other crowded public place and begin drawing the various interesting people you see. It only takes a few moments to realise how varied our proportions and features are. Much of the time I find these on-the-spot sketch sessions very inspiring and great fuel to use in designing my characters back in my studio.

PLAY WITH APPEARANCES

Playing with the endless variations and possibilities of a character's appearance can be quite fun. There are so many ways to push and twist the forms. Of course, how stylised or realistic you want to be will determine the limits of the design to a degree.

It is important to be aware of certain generalisations and psychological triggers when pushing these designs. A huge barrel-chested man with skinny legs and feet can appear clumsy and resemble a goon – which you might want! Tiny eyes set close together can often give the impression of low intelligence. These are not rules set in stone by any means. Having clear intentions, but leaving room for improvisation is usually the most effective way to get the designs you desire.

CHARACTER CREATION

Before I even make any marks on paper, I tend to think of how the new character I am creating compares to a general human. Identify the main differences in scale and proportion.

1. Establish a framework of the figure, concentrating on proportions and the overall shape of the dwarf. Using my intuition, but also making conscious decisions, I draw a head shape, followed by the ribcage. It is a bit of a balancing act. For instance, I naturally make the dwarf top-heavy to give bulk and a sense of strength. When drawing the thin, short legs, I consciously make the feet much larger so they appear to be able to balance the large bulk of the dwarf. I make the arms quite long in proportion, because I felt they appeared stubby and almost useless when too short.

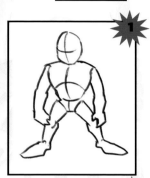

2. At this point, refine the anatomy and features using the framework and proportions already drawn. If I know the character will be clothed, I refrain from including too many details. I only need enough information that will provide a solid base for the rest of the character design.

3. Now with the anatomy in place I can design the armour and clothing suited to the character. The under-drawing will allow the design to be much more accurate and believable.

CHAPTER 3

GENRES

Fantasy art may seem like a genre itself,
but within it there are many other themes
which have become archetypes of the scene.
From Medieval-style landscapes to
heroic steeds and naughty elves, the
artist's imagination can run riot.

FANTASY GENRES

In this section we will go over some of the other important elements that are essential to creating great fantasy art. It is important that you take as much care in improving your skill-set in these areas, as well as the figure. The armour, weaponry and clothing your character wears will say a lot about their personality and intentions. The setting in which your image takes place can determine the mood and atmosphere of your illustration. If your image contains a monster, whether it is good or bad, it should be interesting to look at and well designed.

It can be overwhelming to think of all these things at first when creating an illustration. Isolating these different elements, and practising them individually will make it much easier for you to incorporate them all into one image when you have an idea you want to depict.

LANDSCAPE

One of the most effective ways to transport your viewer to a different world is by creating a convincing environment. It could be a background for your characters and narrative, or it could remain as a landscape painting.

Environments with impact usually make us feel as if we could walk in them. That does not necessarily mean it has to be photo-realism – a good landscape can be very stylised. The atmosphere and mood of the environment should feel very real, regardless of how realistic the manner of the technique is.

Research into exotic places will provide excellent starting points of reference for your fantasy landscapes. Our Earth is filled with so many amazing natural environments that we have an endless supply of inspiration. It could be anything from photos of the rainforests in the Amazon, to a sunset in your local park.

Utopias

The term utopia is very subjective. It could be a lush forest, with running streams and twisted trees. It could also be a seaside city, containing Victorian architecture with an impossible amount of canals and waterways. Anything goes. I find effective illustrations of utopias have a familiarity about them, yet still feel as if they came from a dream. Floating islands and underwater cities may only exist in our imaginations, but by using our artistic skills we can make them very believable. Taking cues from nature and pushing your design will make a very believable and effective illustration of your utopia.

EN PLEIN AIR

A method to enhance your environment paintings is to start doing *plein air* paintings. *En plein air* is a French term that means 'in the open air'. This practice requires you to take your paints out of the studio and set up outdoors and paint from direct observation. Many environment artists who work on commercial films and animations will practice this regularly. There are several advantages to doing *plein air* work that reference from a photo will not replicate. Physically being in the surroundings, and taking in the temperature, smells and atmosphere are all things that are difficult to derive from photo-based reference. The constant light and colour shifts are great things to study, so when it is time to do your fantasy landscape, you will be able to breathe much more life into it.

Left and above Although painting outside can be an invigorating experience, it is often a good idea to take a photograph of the first day you start painting. This means that you are armed against changes to the environment, not to mention changes to the weather, when you will need to move inside.

Right A reliable easel is recommended when you are working outside on a regular basis.

WEAPONS AND ARMOR

Whether your character throws rocks or yields an ax, you should carefully consider the weapons and armor in your illustration. Instead of thinking of the weapons and armor as embellishments of your character, try to think of them as extensions of the characters' personalities and backgrounds. Fantasy art is trying to communicate a narrative within a 2D image, without sounds or words. Being selective and mindful of the weapons and armor is another chance to communicate more information about the image you are creating.

Consider your character's origins and motives. A royal knight's armor will have cohesion and may be more elaborate than a bandit who has pieced together their armor from several sources. A bow and arrow may hint at a character's desire to attack while hidden. A giant ax or hammer will suggest that the character has considerable strength.

The armor and clothing will give insight into the environment the character is from. If the character hails from a cold, mountainous region he or she might wear furs to keep warm. Someone from a warmer climate will be likely to wear lightweight clothing, and far less.

Above Armor for your character could have echoes of modern military design, seen here with the collar and embellished shoulders, or could be thoroughly reimagined with the headwear.

CHARACTER

In the sketch (left) I wanted to give the helmet a strong insectlike appearance. I was inspired by the shape of a rhinoceros beetle, and wanted to mimic the shape a bit in the helmet design. The character also has slightly reptilian eyes, so the armour should reflect that he is not entirely human.

SWORD

In the sword, I was trying to create a unique weapon using various sources and combining them. The handle is heavily influenced by swords used in the American Civil War from the 1860s. The blade is based on a sword shape I saw from the Ottoman Empire from the early nineteenth century. The decorative elements are influence by the Art Nouveau movement at the turn of the twentieth century. All together, they make a completely new weapon that no one has seen before.

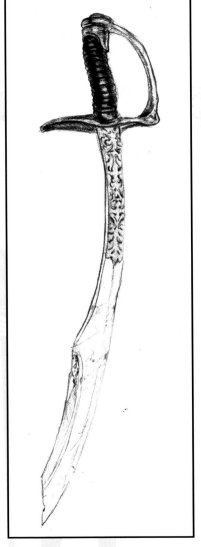

Above A historical sword – reimagined.

MONSTERS

Throughout history, humans have always been captivated by monsters and beasts. Early fairytales and folklore contained creatures such as dragons, centaurs and gargoyles to name a few. While these monsters are still popular, we have a strong desire to always see new monsters created.

Monsters are often used to give an element of fear in a work of art, but they do not always need to be evil. Monsters can be friendly, cute, ugly, huge or tiny – the variables are limitless and will really allow you to flex your creative muscles.

ANIMAL COMBINATIONS

Monsters could be created by combining different elements of existing animals. The ancient Greek

Monster A

mythological beast, the Sphinx, was a human head placed on a lion's body. Even just enlarging an animal can make it appear monstrous. There have been several films with giant bugs, sharks and crocodiles. Insects, in particular, are great inspiration for your monster creations. Many people find them creepy and gross to begin with, so exaggerating and twisting those attributes will only give more power to your monster designs. You are not limited by the constraints of what we see in the natural world, but it is good to observe nature to give believability to your work.

Monster B

COMPARING CREATURES

In these two monsters we see some similarities. They both have two legs, two arms and are standing upright. The joints in their legs are also similar. Monster A's face resembles a human skull, and skulls give an impression of death and creepiness. Even though there is no human for comparison in scale, there is an impression that this creature is very tall, and therefore intimidating.

Monster B has a large head in comparison to its body – much like an infant. We assume this creature is small for this reason, and also because of the attached leaves and flower petals. The big eyes give it an adorable quality, but inversely, the lack of pupils and smile suggest that beyond the cute exterior something sinister awaits.

ARCHETYPES

It is always encouraged in the fantasy art community to push the boundaries of character design and be innovative, yet it is important to identify the genre's archetypes. In a commercial sense, you are often required to depict these archetypes. In an artistic sense, they can help you communicate easily because archetypes act as symbols. Despite being typical of characters in fantasy art, you do not have to worry about creating something generic. The very fact that it is your creation will give it individuality.

Left The inquisitive elf is a modern fantasy archetype.

The heroic warrior:
The archetypal hero is everything a young boy would like to grow up to be. He is tough, strong, agile, quick-witted and excellent in battle. He is muscular like a professional athlete, but not so much that he looks like today's body-builders. The face is ruggedly handsome with a strong jawline.

The grunt, orc, ogre or henchman: The main villain tends to vary quite a bit, but there is always a need for cronies. They are usually big and bulky, so they are quite strong but not as quick as our hero. They lack intelligence and can appear oafish, ugly and beast-like.

The beautiful maiden: She could be a princess or an exceptionally pretty peasant. Her origins are not as important as her appearance. Young and beautiful, she appears almost divine. She is what young girls hope to grow up to be like, and the subject of male desire.

The wizard or sorcerer: This archetype can be portrayed as either good or evil. I have seen just as many noble wizards as I have seen evil sorcerers. They are usually quite elderly, but not completely feeble. Their wisdom is their strength, and of course their ability to conjure magic. They are often depicted wearing modest robes and carrying a staff. The long beard and long hair are common traits of wizards.

CHAPTER 4

ELEMENTS OF DRAWING

Having a confident approach to the technique of drawing is necessary for any art form, especially for working in a fantasy-style which requires a strong sense of realism. This chapter takes you back to the basics, with step-by-step instructions for exploring perspective, texture, composition and portraying light.

TEXTURE

Everything has a texture. From our skin and hair, to the clothes we wear. Identifying the distinct qualities of varying textures in your work will add another dimension to your final piece. It is wise to be cautious of using too much texture, as it can be distracting. Try to be selective in where you use it. I will add texture in areas I want the viewer to focus on, or in areas I feel could use variation to create interest. I will do this if I find an area appears as if it is too uniform and needs to be broken up. Texture can be a great tool for this.

Texture rests on the surface, so it is important to establish the underlying structure and form first. Do not rush into the texture, but reserve it for the later stages of the picture. However, this can also depend on the subject – an object like a tree has such an apparent texture that you should consider it earlier in the process than an object with a more subtle texture like a worn helmet.

CREATING TEXTURE

This will help you to apply texture effectively without sacrificing form. I will use a simple sphere for this demonstration, but the principles can be applied to any object. We will attempt to create an interesting skin texture that may belong to an animal or monster. If we were texturing armour or wood, the process is similar, but the results would be very different. This is a digital step-by-step, but many of the techniques are transferable to traditional methods.

Step 1: Make a decision on where the light is coming from (see pages 89–90) and clearly identify the light and shade. If working traditionally, use a generous amount of white paint, being certain that the values are lighter than the shadows. Digitally, choose lighter values in the colour palette. In both traditional and digital approaches, make sure values that fall in the shadow area are clearly separated from the light area.

Step 2: Start by just indicating some scratches with dark marks. Be mindful of the form. The marks should follow the roundness of the sphere. To make these marks using traditional media, I recommend using a Small Round Brush. Dilute a mixture of a medium–dark value. Keep the paint transparent. The digital approach is similar – use a Small Brush and paint with an opacity setting of 50% or lower.

Step 3: With the darker marks established, indicate where the light would catch the grooves made by these marks. Think of it as a ball of clay and as if you had dug into the surface with a carving tool. Remember to consider the light. The lightest parts of the texture should always follow the light and shade already established. You do not want to make a very light mark in the shadow area as it will disrupt the form.

Step 4: Depending on your image and preference, you could have stopped at Step 3. We will take this a bit further to display how much texture can make a difference to an object. In this step spots are added in various sizes around the form. To add the spots traditionally, take the same approach as you would in Step 2, by applying the paint thinly and using a small brush. Keep the marks random and varied in size. It is important to keep the traditional paint thin, so you do not obliterate the underlying forms. If working digitally, create a new layer for the different steps. This way you can lower the opacity of the layer without having to worry about going too opaque over the object.

Step 5: Raise some hard formations in various sizes around the form. This is good for reptilian, monster and alien skin textures. Many heavy textures rest on top of the form and can give designs a completely different look. To add the formations traditionally, keep using a relatively small brush, but use opaque paint. This also applies to painting digitally – the opacity setting can be as high as 100% if desired.

Step 6: Since these new formations are raised high on the sphere, they will need to have their own light and shade rendered. Be mindful of how the shadows they cast will wrap around the spherical form. Hit the peaks of the bony formations with light, and refine.

ACTION

There are several degrees of action in a scene. We do not always have to depict the peak moment in an action sequence, although when done right it can be extremely effective. Try to find the tension and energy in your piece.

ANATOMY OF CHARACTERS IN ACTION

Before we can produce an action scene, we must first study the human figure in action poses. Study athletes engaged in several sports. Martial arts, boxing, baseball, gymnastics – they are all fantastic sports to study. Your knowledge of anatomy will come in very handy here. Take note of the muscle groups that are working. Push the action in your poses. Even if you think you are pushing the pose too much, chances are you are not. A little exaggeration of the pose can be very effective and create a more dynamic pose. If I am having trouble with an action pose, I will sometimes try out the action myself a few times. This is not necessarily for photographic reference, but just to physically feel the action myself. It helps to feel what is happening to the body, and often helps to translate that to the image.

Left Studying from maquettes and anatomical linework before you begin a loose sketch can help your practice.
Right The human body in action can be an amazing thing to capture – awareness of each muscle contorting and relaxing will add a realism to your work.

Choosing a sequence

Depicting action in a full illustration requires more than just a dynamic figure pose. Identify which moment of the sequence you want to illustrate, whether it is a clash of swords, a tavern brawl or a daring leap.

CREATING ACTION SCENES

There are several ways to get action in your scenes. Often just lowering or raising the viewpoint will add a significant amount of added tension in the illustration. Consider some other devices you can use as we compare these two images.

I wanted to use a simple image, to demonstrate how even small changes can have a big impact on the action in a piece. In both images, the characters are the same. Their eyes are aiming at each other, which is effective. The eye contact establishes a connection between the characters and indicates that they are interacting with each other. Another effective aspect in both images is the movement of hair. Clothing in motion, hair moving, dust being kicked up are all great indicators that action is taking place. These small kinetic factors add up and can help show action in your work.

Illustration 2 (below) has an advantage because it has a tilted horizon line, as well as the characters employing a diagonal direction. This creates a diagonal composition which is much more dynamic than the first image. Even though virtually everything else is the same, the straight horizon line and even placement of the figures creates a very static composition. In some cases you may want this, but for action illustrations this is generally undesirable.

The difference in angle can change how static a piece can seem – motion is much more effective in the illustration above because of the angle of the two figures in relation to the frame and each other.

USING ABSTRACTION

We previously talked about the method of using abstraction to help formulate ideas and spark compositions (see page 38). Using abstraction for a representational painting has far more uses than just this. It can be a great skill to use throughout the entire process.

Although the degree of abstraction you will use depends much on your personal preference and style, every artist uses abstraction to some extent whether they are conscious of it or not. The very idea of a brushstroke representing a tone or the side of a cheek is an artist's attempt at creating realistic results using abstract marks. The culmination of these marks creates a representational image. The closer you get to a painting, the more you can see these abstract brushstrokes and marks, and as you step back the illusion of reality becomes stronger. This is why if you go to museums you will see several people with their noses close to the surface of a painting. They are studying the technique and mark-making that the artist made to create this illusion of reality.

This approach can be used in a multitude of ways. I recommend exploring abstraction in your creative endeavours – from the lush foliage of a forest, to a crowded cityscape.

Texture Overlays in Photoshop

Adding texture is a fantastic way to play with abstraction. What you use as a texture on an Overlay layer is entirely up to you. It can be a photograph, an existing painting, a scanned image – anything! It depends on what you are trying to achieve. Once you have pasted your texture onto an Overlay layer you will want to adjust the opacity on the layer palette. If you want the texture to be very prominent you will have your opacity set closer to 100% and if you want a more subtle effect you will want to lower the opacity. If there are areas you would like to remain textureless you simply need to select the Eraser tool and remove them.

Layers in Photoshop

A knowledge of layers is required as you experiment with abstraction in Photoshop. It will help you avoid making mistakes like changing the original. If you paste anything on a separate layer in Photoshop, whether it is a paper texture, an old painting or a photo – you have several layer modes as options. Each different mode will behave differently when pasting images on the layer, or painting on the layer.

Multiply: This will darken everything on the previous layers, unless white is used on it. That area will not affect the lower layer.

Colour Dodge: This behaves as if you were using the Dodge tool (see page 15), but anything done on this layer will result in greatly lightening the layer beneath it. Nothing done on this layer will darken any part of the image.

Overlay: This mode acts in two ways. Light colours on this will lighten the areas on the previous layers, and darker colours will darken the areas on the previous layers.

Pin Light: I do not use this layer mode that often, but it can often yield unexpected and surprising results. If you paint anything lighter than a middle value on this layer, it will lighten the layer beneath it. If you paint anything darker than a middle value, it will act as a Multiply layer to the layer beneath it.

Colour: This can come in extremely useful when you want to change the colour of a specific area. You can change the colour of a previous layer by painting the desired colour on a Colour layer, without changing the value of the original layer.

Abstraction in finished compositions

In this demonstration I will go over some areas in which using abstraction can be an effective tool in illustration.

In the above provisional image I took some abstract shapes and tried to get the loose impression of a rocky landscape. It is not very defined or resolved yet, but at this stage that is fine. Using the existing shapes I attempt to pull some shapes forwards, push others back and manipulate the image until I achieve my desired result.

To push an object back, I may soften the edges of it by either painting more by using the Smudge tool or Blur tool (see page 16). Another way to push an object back is to paint more of the background colour over it. Inversely, I will bring objects forwards by making their edges crisper, which I do by using a Round Brush with a good amount of pressure.

Adding a figure as a focus, and concentrating the light on her, the piece is in more of a finished state (opposite, top). You can see where I added shadows into the rocks to define them more, but without straying too far from the original abstract shape.

When creating the figure I simply made a new layer in Photoshop and began painting right on top with a Round Brush. I made the figure quite light in value, using very light colours, to bring the figure forwards from the darker background.

Instead of rendering each little crevice and rock, the abstract texture gives the impression that it already exists. If you were to render each pebble your image would lose the main focus and look a bit boring. By mixing up areas of more polished rendering, as in the figure and focal points, and areas that are looser and abstract, you achieve a much more interesting image. It also gives the viewer a subconscious ability to rest the eyes in certain places and bounce around the image. I tried to maintain a lot of the texture achieved in the abstract method, which you can see in the detail images (see right).

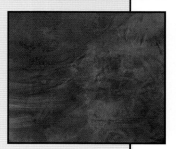

GOOD COMPOSITION

Composition is often discussed in artistic circles as an elusive idea that is difficult to teach. One of my professors, during my years as an illustration major, once told our class, 'If your composition is interesting, then it works.' I believe this to be true for the most part. Throughout art history we have seen very daring cropping and unusual placement in compositions that have resulted in great imagery. It is okay to take chances in your compositions, and there are almost no restrictions in what you can do, as long as you find a way to make it work.

Despite having an open arena to create your images, composition continues to be one of the most difficult aspects for many artists. It helps to have a compositional concept in mind. It can be anything regarding your illustration. Perhaps you have an idea that the image will be lit by two light sources, or that the image will be very dark, or you will have large shapes in the foreground and open area in the background. This can change as you work on your image, but I find it useful to have a starting point.

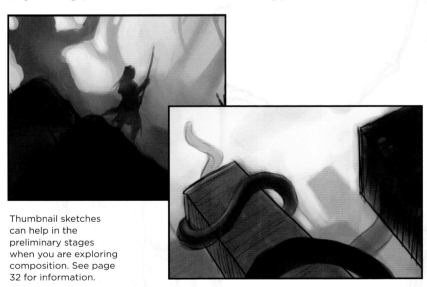

Thumbnail sketches can help in the preliminary stages when you are exploring composition. See page 32 for information.

MOVEMENT AND CROPPING

In several of my illustrations, I like to establish a sense of movement. This does not always mean I am creating action (although sometimes it does) but more a sense of the direction I want to take the viewers' eyes in. One thing I like to do is use elements of the painting to assist in this direction. It can be a tree branch pointing at the focal point, or a big rock or building that stops the viewers' eyes from leaving the intended areas of interest. One thing to make a note of is the cropping of human limbs. Interesting cropping is encouraged, but avoid cropping a figure, creature or animal at any joint. It will not appear as creative cropping, but more of an amputation.

Playing with different crops can alter the mood and composition of your piece.

COMPOSITION AND MOVEMENT

In this composition I wanted to establish a diagonal movement. The diagonal direction helps move the viewer towards one of the main focal points – the creature. Note how the humans' weapons are pointed at the creature and they are all facing in his direction. I also used the rocks to assist in this movement, and pointed many of them in the creature's direction as well.

I also aimed to establish a clear concept of chromatic structure. In simple terms, I wanted a clear hierarchy of intense colour, compared to very subdued colour. The majority of the painting is in very muted tones, except the central human figure with the red cape, and the creature whose eyes, mouth and ears are also in more intense hues.

The compositional idea was very simple, but sometimes that does not have to be a negative thing. Often, simplifying your ideas and concepts will make your composition much stronger.

LIGHT AND MOOD

There are many different types of lighting variables and they all have different effects on the image. A scene lit by candlelight will appear dark and very moody. Take the same scene and use daylight from the window to illuminate the scene. The scene will appear lighter, softer and inviting. Do not make the lighting an after-thought in your creation; it should be an integral decision.

It is wise to study visual art for various lighting options, but I find it helpful to study light from film or photography as well. Directors employ light technicians who spend their whole career working on the best spotlights and tones so it is an illuminating way to perfect your craft. As much as we can learn about studio lighting, nature will always provide unpredictable and interesting lighting scenarios.

Adding light sources digitally and traditionally

There are only a few ways to add light when painting. You will need to mix a lighter value colour than the area you are applying then paint over. Usually you will mix white into the new colour, but any lighter paint can work, such as Naples yellow light. When applying highlights, it is easier to use thicker, more opaque paint.

If the paint is still wet, you can sometimes lighten the area by wiping out the selected area with a cloth. This will only lighten the selected portion if the area beneath it is lighter. You can also use the sharper point of a palette knife to scratch away areas of paint. This can be risky, because if you scratch too hard you may damage the surface of your painting. Be careful.

There are a few more ways to lighten digitally. Simply using a Regular Round Brush and a lighter colour will lighten the area on a Normal layer. If the area on the previous layer is lighter, you can also use your Eraser to expose the lighter section in the top layer of the painting. The Overlay and Colour Dodge layers are also very effective in lightening areas (see page 81 for information about the way they work). You can also use the Dodge tool to lighten any areas (see page 15).

LIGHTING SCENARIOS AND THEIR EFFECTS

Lighting can have a profound effect on the way the subject appears and also on the mood of a piece. It is good to familiarise yourself with some basic lighting scenarios – these lighting set-ups are good examples to start with.

1. This is overhead lighting. Depending on the source, it can vary in its softness or hardness. Direct overhead lighting is often caused by artificial lighting, when your scene is located indoors. It tends to cause harsh shadows, which may be your desired effect, although it can make faces look harsher than you intend them to. As for establishing form, it is very effective.

2. This lighting goes by several names. It is often referred to as 'portrait lighting' because it is optimal for portraiture and is very good for establishing form. It is also known as 'Rembrandt lighting' because it is often found in his work. The term '³/₄ lighting' describes it best – ³/₄ of the face is in light, while the rest is caught in shade. This gives a gradient light with a full range of values, which makes it clear to see the forms.

3. Backlighting can be very atmospheric, yet it proves a little more difficult to establish form. The term describes it fully – the subject is lit from the back. This causes the subject to be in shadow, so a secondary light source is sometimes needed. Since much of the subject is cast in shadow you must observe the value shifts very carefully. The changes will be much more subtle.

4. Dual lighting is caused by a subject being lit by two light sources. Often it will be set up with one natural light source, such as a sunlit window, and an artificial light source.

The Swedish master, Anders Zorn (1860–1920) used this technique in a lot of his successful portraits.

Imaginative use of light

In this illustration, we have a young lady with some glowing leaves. There are no dragons, castles or knights on horseback, yet the image still evokes the themes of fantasy art. This is due to the lighting, and the mood being created by this light. Fantasy art can explore lighting situations you would never see in the real world. Fantasy art can be an intensified reality, and the lighting should reflect this.

To get the leaves to have a slight 'glow' is fairly simple to do digitally. The leaves were already very light, but to give them more glow I added a new layer and set the mode as Overlay. Then, using a Soft Round Brush, I selected a light yellow and painted over the leaves and around the edges. You do not need to use white – just a light value. You can control the colour of the glow by selecting different colours – a blue colour will give a cooler glow, while a light red might give you a pinkish glow.

A dreamlike image is achieved with the use of glowing light and contrasting colours.

CHAPTER 5

FUNDAMENTALS

Fantasy art requires a lot of the artist. Armour, weapons, characters, monsters, environments - it can be very overwhelming to beginners. In fact, it can be very overwhelming for advanced artists too! There is quite a range of diverse subject matters and mastery of it all seems impossible. Whether it is a sword or a winged demon, the basic fundamentals will allow you to transfer all of your ideas to paper or canvas.

THE FUNDAMENTALS

Many of us start out just drawing from our imagination as children, without any prior instruction. At some point we get the desire to be able to clarify our thoughts and push the boundaries of what we can do with our pencils and brushes. It may be what prompted you to pick up this book. These fundamental art skills will bring you closer to that goal – take the time to hone these skills. They will open new doors for your creativity.

FORESHORTENING

As representational painters, our job is to create a 3D image on a 2D surface. Rendering a form with proper light and shade will help this, but we often need to foreshorten subjects. Foreshortening is used when an object or form is moving towards the viewer, creating an optical illusion that the object's size has altered. In reality, the shape or object does not change size or dimension. On our paper, we must accurately convey what we see to create the illusion of space. The closer the object is to us, the bigger it will get, and the further away it goes back in space the smaller it will appear.

Foreshortening can be tricky, as forms get distorted and do not appear as we expect them to. If a foot is coming at us, the foot may seem very large, while the legs – usually the longest part of the body – appear short. Observing from nature and proper reference will assist you. Be sure to trust what you see, and do not try to make the shapes fit what you believe they should be.

It can be a bit of a struggle to become comfortable with foreshortening, but when done correctly it can add a whole other dimension and dynamic quality to your imagery.

Simple shapes with foreshortening

A good way to simplify some of the complexity that occurs with foreshortening is to break down the forms into simpler shapes. Let us say you wanted to have a hand coming at the viewer. Simplify the arm and hand by thinking of the forms as cylinders. As the cylinder comes towards you, the shapes increase in size, and as they go back in space they diminish in size. Also note which shapes are now in front of the other. The hand will block a portion of the forearm and perhaps more, depending on the position and viewpoint.

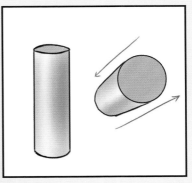

Above The cylindrical method of simplifying your figure will help you gauge the correct size.

Above As the hand comes towards you, it increases in size.

USE OF REFERENCE

We previously talked about acquiring useful reference for your imagery. Aside from the reference materials we find in our research, you will often need to take photographs to create your own reference material. All artists use reference to varying degrees, depending on their style and goals. Regardless of how realistic you want your images to be, you should always be ready to take reference when the need arises.

YOUR SET-UP

All that is needed is a very simple set-up. If your style depends on reference more strongly, you will want a more elaborate set-up. For my needs, I keep it very basic: a camera, tripod and a portable light source. Often you will need to simulate clothing, armour and weapons. You can find several places to rent costumes and these materials. Many times you can improvise with materials in your home. Be creative and remember that the reference is just that... a reference point. There is still a lot of work and problem-solving to do even after that point.

In the studio

In this piece, I wanted to get a realistic feel for the body and the folds in the clothing, so the surreal elements would stand out more. The clothing was easy, as it was modern clothing someone could find in their closet. I set up the model against the wall and moved my light to get the desired result. Remember you are in control. Get the scene to look as close to your vision as you can.

I also continue working on reference material after photo shoots. First, I almost always convert the photo to greyscale. I like to reduce the amount of information in the photo, so I can just concentrate on the values. I also feel this makes me think more about colour and be more creative. I often will paint digitally on top of the photo reference to try things out before I start on the painting itself. This can save a lot of time, and help visualise the final image.

Digitally painting over your reference can help you visualise your paintings, whether they are traditional or digital. Using reference even in unrealistic fantasy settings can help add a level of realism and believability to your imaginative imagery.

APPLYING TONES AND VALUE

Throughout this book you have seen the term 'values' mentioned numerous times. That is because understanding values is one of the essential fundamentals you can learn in your artistic foundation. Simply, value is how light or how dark something is. Everything can be assigned a value, from the sky to the shirt you are wearing.

To apply tones, you first need to acknowledge the value. In some situations the value structure can be quite staggering, which is why it is a good idea to have a process when applying tones. Think of values and tones as levels of dark and light that can be assigned on a greyscale. Colour can interfere with how we see values. A very bright red shirt may appear brighter than it really is, so it will take some practice to train your eyes.

AN EXERCISE WITH TONES

A sphere lit by a single light source is a good starting point.

1. To apply tones, you must first break down the subject into light and shade. Try to find where the light stops and the shadow begins. In some cases it will be very clear; in others it will be more subtle.

2. After you distinguish the light and shade, you can begin applying the rest of the tones. All surfaces and lighting conditions will vary, but if we look at our sphere we can identify what we should look for.

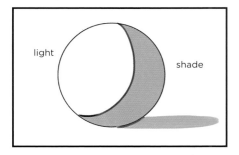

light

shade

A glossary of terms

Terminator: This is where the light and shadow meet, and is usually the darkest part of the shadow aside from the accents.

Half-tone: This is the transitional area from the shade into the light. The more gradual the turn of the form, the more half-tone there is. An object with a sharp edge in light and shade – like a box – will have little or no half-tone.

Reflected light: This happens when light bounces back into the shadow. There is usually some degree of reflected light, unless the subject is in a cave.

Cast shadow: This is the shadow cast on the surrounding surfaces from the object.

Highlight: The brightest part in the light.

Accent: The absolute darkest part of the shadow.

Everything in the light should be lighter in value than everything in the shadow. Even the lightest part of the shadow should still remain darker than the darkest part of the light.

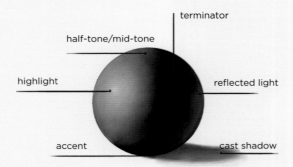

terminator

half-tone/mid-tone

highlight

reflected light

accent

cast shadow

EXAGGERATION

Exaggeration has been used by animators and cartoonists for years. You can exaggerate a character's ugliness by making the features grotesquely disproportionate. To exaggerate a character's imposing physical presence, you can make the scale larger than normal. Depending on what you want to achieve with your exaggeration, you can manipulate proportions and forms as much as your vision dictates. Pushing forms beyond their norms can be more than just a stylistic choice. It can give your designs more life and your figures more energy.

Caricature also utilises exaggeration. Distorting the features of a person to capture their essence on paper is a common use of exaggeration. If someone has very large lips, make them larger. If they have very skinny legs, make them even skinnier. The challenge is getting all the exaggerated features to still synch up to capture the likeness of the person.

Left Exaggerating facial features like a grin and a bulbous nose can add character and humour to a figure – or indeed grotesque horror, depending on the treatment.

Be playful

I particularly like using a good amount of exaggeration in my more whimsical creature designs. A playful approach will keep things fun for you, and that is when the work begins to feel effortless.

In this gnome's face, I have enlarged the nose and chin. I also exaggerated the small distance between the nose and mouth by making it even smaller. By making the eyes very small and the forehead small, the exaggerated features appear even larger.

Above Experiment with your figures until you get the best combination of features.

REFLECTIONS AND SURFACE

There are countless materials in the world, all of which have unique properties that respond differently to light. Observing objects and studying them will enrich your visual vocabulary, and give you insight on how to render these objects. As fantasy artists, we will not only observe what we see, but understand why we see it.

This need will arise when constructing your images. Perhaps you have a knight who you want standing next to a big red dragon. Even with good reference of a knight in armour, there will still be elements missing. What happens to the armour when a big, bright red dragon is nearby? Because of the armour's metallic surface, the red colour will likely show up in the metal. Understanding the inherent qualities of different materials will help you add realism to your work. More importantly, it will unify the different elements of your picture, so they appear as if they exist in the same world.

Left There are always far more than two colours on a reflective surface.

An exercise in reflection

This is a slightly worn, metallic helmet. The surface is shiny, so we have many more highlights and darks compared to human flesh with the same lighting. Metallic surfaces also respond greatly to surroundings, as we can see in the combination below.

Placing the red ball next to the helmet, we can observe how the red ball's strong red colour shows up in the helmet. If you look in the red ball's shadow, you can see how there is a slight purplish hue, bouncing back onto the surface. If the ball was metallic, the purplish hue would be much more apparent.

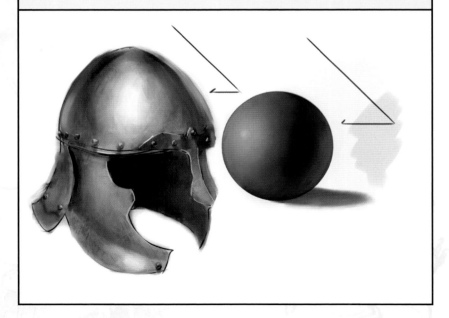

APPLYING COLOUR

Colour is a great way to express your individuality in your work. The endless possibilities and combinations of colours give us a good deal of creative freedom in our palette choices. We can choose to use very natural colours, over-saturated colours, muted colours and even wacky, crazy colours. It is our application that will determine if our colours work in our illustrations.

There are several methods for applying colour, both traditionally and digitally. Some artists prefer to just go direct in full colour right from the beginning. Others prefer to establish the values first and apply colour afterwards.

Establishing values using Photoshop

I have painted a human head in greyscale. To do this in Photoshop, I simply used a Round Brush and a Small Chalk Brush for a bit of texture. This allows me to just concentrate on the values, lighting and form without having to worry about colour at this stage. When I arrive at a point where I think the drawing and structure looks good, I will then proceed to colour.

Create a new Colour layer. Using a Soft Round Brush begin painting over the greyscale image with selected colours. Note the colour and temperature shifts. The ears and nose tend to be warmer in colour, because there is more blood flow there. Around the mouth and jaw of the face, the colour becomes more neutral or cooler because of facial hair. Once colours are established, you can begin to refine your imagery.

Establishing values using oil paints

This uses a similar technique to the digital head, but using traditional oil paints. Using thinned out Raw umber (using a small amount of Turpenoid and linseed oil), block in the values and basic drawing. The paint is applied heavily in the darker areas, while being wiped out with a rag in the lighter areas. Once this under-painting is complete, let it dry. During the next painting session, begin by thinly applying colour on top of the under-painting, slowly getting thicker as you proceed to the later stages. See page 128 for detailed steps to under-painting.

COLOUR THEORY

The first thing to grasp about colour theory is the basics. An understanding of the primary and secondary colours may be basic, but the applications of this can be very advanced.

The primary colours are red, blue and yellow. These colours cannot be created from mixing other colours. To create the secondary colours you simply need to mix two primary colours.

Red + Blue = Purple
Blue + Yellow = Green
Red + Yellow = Orange

Purple, green and orange are the secondary colours. The secondary colours also make up the complementary colours. Complementary colours are hues that are opposite each other on the colour wheel. For example, blue and orange complement each other. This information can become extremely valuable in creating your images. They can helpful when mixed together, or when juxtaposed next to each other.

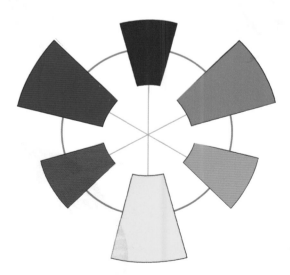

Looking at our red ball, I have placed it against its complementary colour, green. This helps the ball stand out, or 'pop' – a term often used in illustration. Mixing the complementary green in the shadow and half-tone of the red ball also helps to create the illusion that the form is 'turning' – which means that the 3D illusion is taking place.

WARM AND COOL HUES

Another important aspect of colour theory is the separation of warm and cool colours. Think of colours you associate with these sensations. The sun and fire we normally think of in terms of red, orange and yellow. Ice and snow we think of in blues and light purples. Warms and cool are not limited to these hues, as you can create varying degrees of warmth or coolness in any colour.

Hues in action

This image utilises both complementary colours and the effects of temperature in hues. The bulk of the image is made up of warm green hues, with plenty of yellow mixed in. To create the cooler green hues, more blue was added. The complement of yellow tones is purple, which is being used to help define the form, especially where the light meets the shadow areas. It can create a much more interesting picture when you start using temperature shifts in hues. Not only is it visually pleasing, but it can add a lot of life to your work.

CHAPTER 6

CREATING WORLDS

Fantasy art's intention is to bring the viewer into a different world. Even if that world mirrors that of our own, it is a more intense version of the one we live in. Sometimes that world will be removed from our world, but there will always be some parallels to what we've known. Without these parallels, we have nothing to associate ourselves with. The key is to take elements from our world and use them to make our new creations believable.

CREATING WORLDS

n some cases, thinking of the world you would like to set your artwork in will help you flesh out the characters and narrative of your illustrations. Once the world is created, you can almost conclude from the environment what kind of humans and creatures would live there. It is much like seeing an animal in its natural habitat – it looks like it belongs there. The conditions will affect how characters dress, and you can imagine what kind of creature would evolve there efficiently. You get to become a fantasy scientist of sorts. The difference is, instead of simply observing the specimens, you are creating them.

HYPER REALITY

What would you like your world to be? Would it be more playful with brighter colours and softer shapes? Would giant rocks float in the air as if they were weightless? These decisions are all up to you. The key to hyper reality is to push your imagination beyond the boundaries of what we see in everyday life. If you decide you want to make a forest with large, twisted trees, make them larger and more twisted than normal. If you would like a city with magnificently ornate architecture, make the most beautiful city you could ever imagine.

DISTORTION

In essence, hyper reality is somewhat of an illusion. We are taking what we know of the real world, and distorting it somehow to make it more desirable, intense or visually pleasing. Creating something that we cannot achieve in our reality is the ultimate goal of hyper reality.

Abstraction and hyper reality

In this illustration, the environment is just one solitary rocky formation, floating in ambiguous space. The tree has unusual spherical formations for leaves, yet we still understand it to be a tree. If our eyes explore the image in detail we can start to see an odd face emerging from the rocky structure.

Left There are a number of qualities in the image which make you want to explore. The tree is almost naturalistic but not quite, with its round, unrecognisable growths; the rocks look like mountain ranges but they have been distorted.

PERSPECTIVE

Out of all the skills I can think of, perspective seems to come the least naturally to the majority of artists. It can be fairly technical and even mathematical at times. If you are doing an organic environment design, such as a forest or mountain region, you have a little bit more flexibility and can follow a looser perspective. If you want to do an environment containing architecture, such as a village or cityscape, your perspective will need to be much more accurate. It is very important you learn about perspective, so learn the basics either way.

ONE-POINT PERSPECTIVE

As its name would lead you to believe, there is only one vanishing point in one-point perspective. To create a simple one-point perspective guide, first draw your horizon line. The horizon line is the line that indicates where the sky meets land. You can pick anywhere on this horizon line, and place your vanishing point there. From this point, all perspective lines will radiate, and all guidelines lead to this vanishing point.

Although simple, one-point perspective can be effective as the viewer's eye will naturally look towards the vanishing point. Here, you can use your one-point perspective to guide the viewer into the piece.

Perspective takes practice and constant study. Start with simple shapes like the cubes you see here. Once you feel comfortable, you can attempt more complicated shapes.

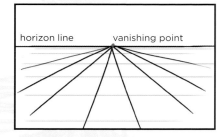

horizon line   vanishing point

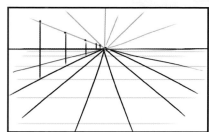

TWO-POINT PERSPECTIVE

This is probably the most commonly used perspective in creating environments. Instead of one point, there are now two points on the horizon line. The perspective lines will now intersect each other, giving you a great guide for your environment. Be sure to place your two points an ample distant apart. If they are too close, you will get distortion that will look odd. It is common to place one vanishing point outside the picture plane so this does not occur.

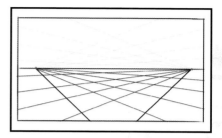

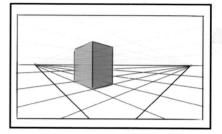

THREE-POINT PERSPECTIVE

Three-point perspective can be more complicated. There are two main applications for three-point perspective.

The first is what we call 'bird's eye view' (right) where you are looking down from a higher point. In this case, you would want to place a third point beneath the horizon line.

The second is what is referred to as 'worm's eye view' (right) which is when you are looking up from a lower point. Here, you will place the third point above the horizon line.

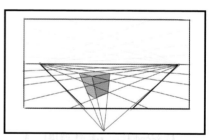

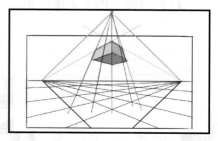

ATMOSPHERIC PERSPECTIVE

Atmospheric perspective has less to do with vanishing points, and more to do with the visual effects of objects receding back in space. To create this illusion, imagine you are painting air, and the more space that is between you and an object, the more air you will need to paint. There are some general rules that are good to follow for atmospheric perspective.

1. The further away something is, the less contrast there will be. Objects closer to you will have greater contrast in light and dark, but as objects recede further in the distance the values become closer together.

2. Intensity of colour is greatly reduced the further it is in the distance. Even the brightest red shirt will be significantly brighter close to the foreground than it will be in the distant background.

3. Objects are sharper and clearer in the foreground. As objects go further into the background, they become less sharp and more out of focus.

Save the details for objects closer to you, and reduce detail in objects further away. This will help create the illusion of space, and also help avoid the pitfall of having an image with too much detail.

ENVIRONMENTS

Great environmental design is more sought out today than ever before. Not only has technology allowed the film industry to create bigger and more elaborate worlds, but the video game requires great environments as well. Games are much more immersive and gamers desire new worlds to explore. This has influenced fantasy-art illustration, as we are now seeing even better environment designs in 2D work as well.

When creating your environments, try to establish some focal points as you would for an illustration with characters. Even if there are no figures at all, it will help give the illustration focus and keep it from becoming scattered. If you are concerned with establishing scale, whether it be mountains or buildings, try placing a few figures in the environment so we can clearly see the relation in size.

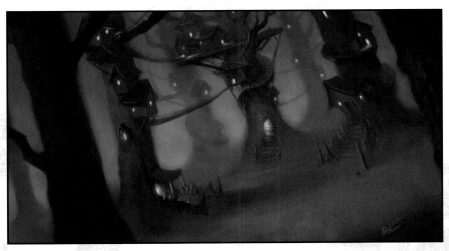

Above The steps from the trees help establish the trees' placement in relation to each other.

USING OLD ARCHITECTURE

This environment is steampunkish and futuristic. I decided that I wanted it to appear as if there was an old city beneath the new architecture, as if it was a city that was being updated and modified as opposed to brand new shiny buildings. It was mostly inspired by gothic architecture, even though the environment belongs to a time far into the future. I felt the image needed something to bring the viewers in so I suggested a train system throughout the city. I used this opportunity to bring in some bright cool hues on the lights, to break up the overall golden rusty palette of the image.

I often start my environment work with some preliminary work, such as thumbnails, drawings or colour sketches (see page 30–33). Environments can get pretty complex, so I like to have a firm grasp on the underlying structure before I dive into the final painting. Some are created in greyscale, so I can understand the values first, and then I produce a colour sketch to grasp the light and hues of the rocky environment.

Above The use of gothic architecture with a futuristic twist adds to the feeling of hyper reality and dystopia.

THE ART OF SIMPLICITY

Consistently throughout this book you have seen the word simplify. When you want to create a complicated image, like an elaborate environment, it helps to simplify everything down to its basic structure. Add on top of the simplified structure, using it as a foundation for your details, but it does not work in reverse. The structure must be there before the details are included.

BUILDING UP THE EFFECTS

In this environment step-by-step, establishing large shapes at the beginning is such a help. Once I have simplified correctly, the image almost paints itself.

Step 1: Create these large shapes using a Large Round Brush. Notice how simple these shapes are. We can already get an idea of the perspective and that there are man-made structures receding into the distance.

Step 2: More shapes for the rock formations on the side of the image have been added. They are still very basic in shape, and do not include detail. Use the shape to start defining the man-made structure in the middle of the composition.

Step 3: The areas of interest have started to be more refined, while adding a bit more definition to the structures and rock formations.

Step 4: At the last stage begin tweaking the levels and colour. Start adding more texture to give a better sense of the material there. A bit more detail is added and I polish the image off.

Adjusting Levels and Colour Balance

In the Levels palette in Photoshop there are three different levels that you can adjust – Black, Grey and White. You may just decide to move the middle grey slider to the right – towards the white slider. Just a slight adjustment will darken the middle values, and you will also see a slight increase in saturation. Move the white slider slightly to the left (towards the grey slider) and that makes the lighter values even lighter. To darken the very darkest areas, move the black slider slightly towards the right.

In the Colour Balance palette you will notice three areas to adjust the colour on the bottom of the palette: Shadows, Midtones and Highlights. I like to start with the Midtones; this will affect all areas that have a value between the Shadows and Highlights. Move the slider towards the Magenta and it will add more pinks and purples into your colour. Move the slider more towards yellow and you will see more yellow hues appear in your painting. You may want, for flexibility, to only adjust the Colour Balance in the shadows or highlights.

CHAPTER 7

PROJECTS
BASIC TECHNIQUES
AND MATERIALS

The following pages will help you to achieve the very best results from the step-by-step projects - from the best materials, to the techniques which crop up frequently.

PROJECT MATERIALS

Before we go in-depth with the projects, this section will cover the drawing supplies to keep readily available. I do all my sketching and drawing with these. While it is always wise to try different media, it is important to have a staple selection of reliable materials for you to grab at a moment's notice.

Drawing materials

Col-Erase pencils are very common for animators and comic book artists. They are waxier than normal graphite, and harder to erase, but they make lighter marks that graphite goes over very well. You can also do an under-drawing and remove the Col-Erase blue lines by turning off the Blue layer in the Channels palette in Photoshop.

Use a combination of mechanical and regular wooden pencils. With regular wooden pencils you can use the side to get broad strokes and achieve a greater variety of tones. I usually use HB, B, F and 2B. I use mechanical pencils that take 0.5mm and 0.7mm graphite. For the majority of the time I use the 0.5mm, as is great for drawing on location or when not in the studio. I usually keep HB or F graphite in the 0.5mm pencil. The 0.7mm behaves more like a regular pencil, but does need a special sharpener. I usually keep a softer graphite inside the 0.7mm, such as 2B or 6B.

Charcoal can be a good medium to work in if you prefer a more 'painterly' approach. I will usually start off with compressed or vine charcoal and make broad strokes, much like I start an oil painting. For finer detail I will use a charcoal pencil – either a 2B or a 6B. If I am working on a toned surface I like to use a white pencil for highlights.

The eraser I use the most is a kneaded eraser. It can be moulded to fit small areas, and is also good for larger sections. It can also be cleaned just by 'kneading' it for a minute. The harder eraser comes in handy when you want to completely obliterate a section.

One of my favourite drawing tools is a simple ballpoint pen. They are easy to find, and inexpensive. They deliver crisp lines and you can achieve a surprisingly broad range of values just by applying and decreasing pressure.

fig. 1

fig. 2

fig. 3

fig. 4

fig. 5

fig. 6

fig. 7

1. & 2. Col-Erase pencils
3. 0.5mm mechanical pencil
4. Charcoal pencil
5. Ballpoint pen
6. Kneaded eraser
7. Hard eraser

OIL PAINTING MATERIALS

Some basic materials are covered on page 11, but here are my recommendations for basic materials specific to oil painting – my traditional medium of choice.

1. Use a wood palette or a glass palette. I keep my palette organised in a way that is familiar to me and I do not have to search for colours. My palette does go through adjustments from time to time, but this list is what I normally keep available to me.

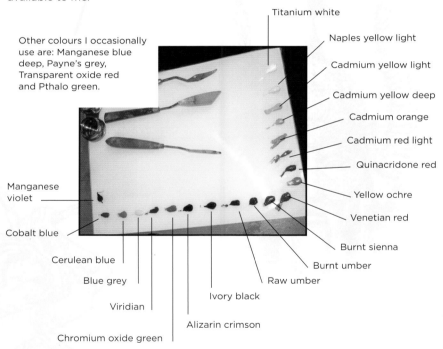

Titanium white

Other colours I occasionally use are: Manganese blue deep, Payne's grey, Transparent oxide red and Pthalo green.

Naples yellow light

Cadmium yellow light

Cadmium yellow deep

Cadmium orange

Cadmium red light

Quinacridone red

Yellow ochre

Venetian red

Burnt sienna

Burnt umber

Raw umber

Ivory black

Alizarin crimson

Chromium oxide green

Viridian

Blue grey

Cerulean blue

Cobalt blue

Manganese violet

2. I keep a large stash of brushes at my disposal. They are the extensions of your hands and direct contact to make the marks you want. It is good to be able to have a variety of these tools for a variety of situations. I mostly use flat bristle brushes for pushing around large areas of paint. You can also load quite a bit of paint on a bristle brush and achieve good impasto effects. For more subtle areas, I will use synthetic brushes, which hold less paint. I like to use brights, which are the same shape as flats, just shorter. For edgework, blending and thin passages I will use sable brushes. For detailed work I use watercolour sables, in sizes 0 or 00.

3. Detail brushes must retain their points. Many small brushes will fray quickly and be useless for details. I also like to use a fan brush to drag broken colour over passages during the later stages.

4. Palette knives can be used as brushes, especially when you have different sizes of them. There is an element of unpredictability about them that I quite like. They are great for heavy texture and impasto effects, but also good for scraping areas to reveal underlying layers.

5. In oil painting you will want a thinner such as turpentine or turpenoid to dilute your paint. They are both clear in appearance, but turpentine has a much stronger odour. There are several mediums available to mix with the paint out of the tube to achieve a more manageable consistency. One of the most widely used and preferred is cold-pressed linseed oil. If you are looking for something to speed up the drying time of your painting, Liquin is a good medium to use. There are other options such as Galkyd, Japan Drier and Cobalt Drier. Experiment and use what works best for you.

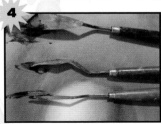

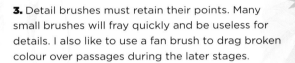

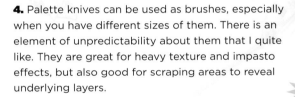

UNDER-PAINTING WIPE-OUT METHOD

This step-by-step will go through my process of creating an under-painting in traditional oil paint. This method is extremely useful in acting as a guide to the painting, and the underlying layer will also help add a more dimensional quality to your work.

Step 1: With a clean rag or lint-free cloth, dip the end into linseed oil. Then rub the entire painting surface to give a very slight coat of linseed oil. It should be just a trace amount and not dripping wet.

Step 2: The colours you will use will depend on how neutral or warm you want your under-painting to be. For this under-painting I used a mixture of raw umber and just a tiny amount of Ultramarine blue. With a large sable brush cover the entire canvas with the diluted paint.

Step 3: Now that the entire surface is toned, take a small bristle flat brush and with the same paint mixture begin drawing in the subject. The drawing only needs to be very simple and functional.

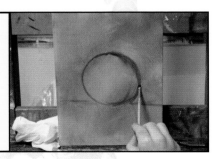

Step 4: Using a fairly large sable flat, start blocking in the major shadow shapes, using the same paint mixture. Where the shadows are darker, add more pigment, and use less in lighter areas.

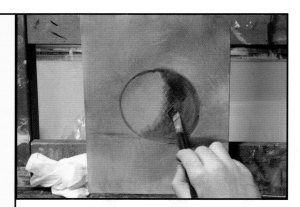

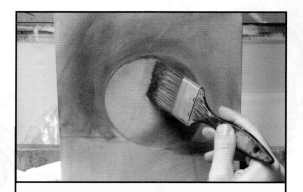

Step 5: During the entire process constantly use a large brush to soften edges and blend the tones together until you get the desired result. It is a similar approach to sculpting with paint as you try to mould the forms.

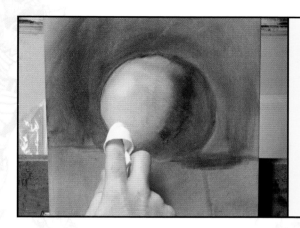

Step 6: To achieve lighter values, you subtract paint by wiping away pigment with a rag. Apply more pressure when you want to wipe away more and achieve even lighter values.

Step 7: Using just one colour and wiping out the lights, you can achieve a good range of values that sets up the painting for the next layers. You can let the under-painting show through to achieve interesting effects with colour and texture.

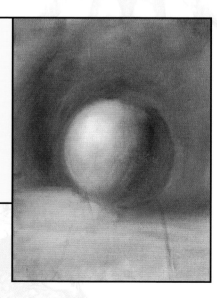

WATERCOLOUR PAPER TEXTURES

Throughout this book you will see I am constantly using texture overlays in my digital work, and often they are watercolour paper textures I have made myself. They are fun and easy to make, and you can experiment with many different approaches to get interesting results. I find they bring a more organic look to my digital paintings as well as helping to unify the entire image.

Step 1: Use fairly inexpensive watercolour paper for these textures, since they are meant to be quick. You should not be concerned with doing polished work on them. I find 250 gsm cold pressed watercolour paper works well. Start off using a large brush and apply a thin coat of water evenly over the paper.

Step 2: Using a large synthetic sable brush, lightly wet your brush and pick up some pigment from your watercolours and quickly brush across the entire paper.

I sometimes blend several colours. You can also just keep it fairly monochromatic depending on what you want to achieve.

Step 3: Experiment and try new things with paper textures. One way to get interesting effects is while the paper is still wet, sprinkle some salt onto the painting. Be sure to let the painting fully dry before you brush off the salt.

Step 4: When the paper is fully dry brush off the salt. The results will usually be unique. You could choose to keep working on the same texture paper or leave it as is. Sometimes you may only want a texture of a watercolour wash. Build a texture library of many different textures for different uses.

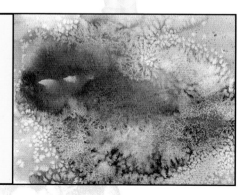

Step 5: Another great way to get interesting textures is by using a can of compressed gas that is used to clean electrical devices. Create a small puddle-like blob with water and pigment. Then proceed to blow the puddle around to create interesting effects.

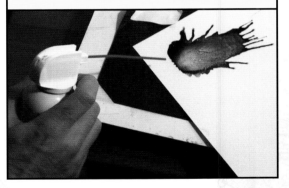

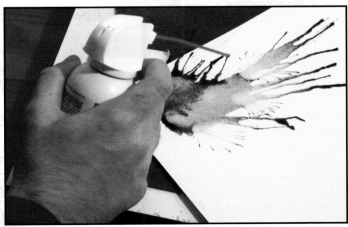

Step 6: This is a technique I picked up from comic book artists. Use an old toothbrush and load it with pigment. Then using a brush handle or even your thumb, pull back the bristles on the brush and as they spring back they will flick pigment onto the paper. This can create really interesting splatter effects that make for great texture overlays.

PROJECTS
WEAPONS AND ARMOUR

The right weapons and armour can take an average battle scene and transform it into something amazing. Try combining aspects from different eras with elements from the natural world to create unexpected masterpieces in feudal design.

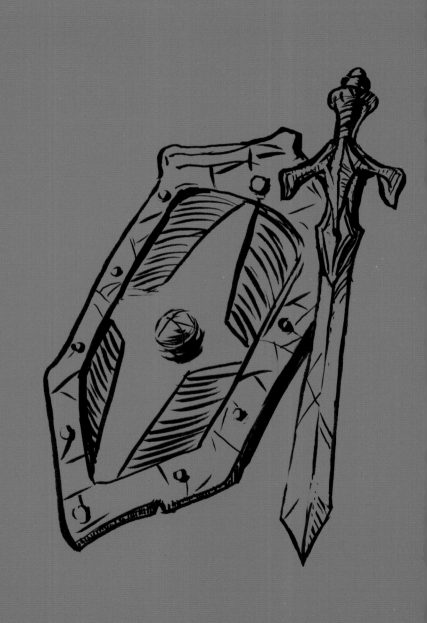

ARMOUR SET

This project was created using Photoshop. It could be done using traditional methods, but it could take much longer because the symmetrical design would require you to trace one half of the image, flip it and then copy the mirrored image so it connects to the other half.

Step 1: Using a Round Brush, establish a very general torso for a male. This gives a strong structure. I make sure the viewpoint is straight on so I can build the design with digital tools.

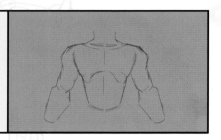

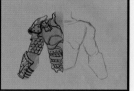

Step 2: Draw a line down the centre of the torso. Using a Hard Round Brush, draw on only one half of the armour set. Even at the drawing stage, pay close attention to the different materials – try to mix it up with smooth areas against an area with a texture. This goes the same for areas that provide functionality, like buckles and straps, against areas that provide ornamentation for visual interest. Add a grey wash using a Large Brush.

Step 3: Select the one half of the drawing using the Lasso tool. Then choose Edit>Transform>Flip Horizontal, to get a mirror image. Use the Move tool, which is the black arrow at the very top of the Tool Bar, and piece the two mirrored sides together.

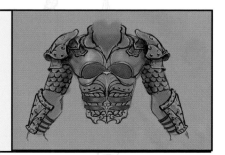

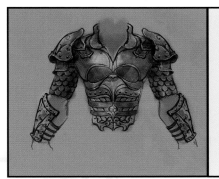

Step 4: Instead of metal I wanted this armour to be made of a hard shell covered in tough leather. On a Colour layer, start adding rusty blues and oranges, separating different sections of the armour to assist with the designs. Add a subtle texture overlay (see page 80) to give a worn and weathered appearance.

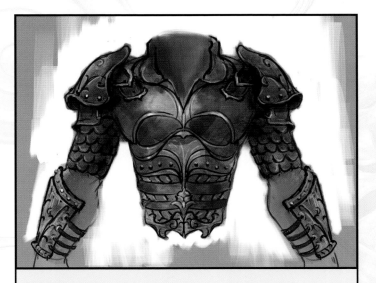

Step 5: Separate the armour from the background – use a Square Brush and place a white area around the focus. Add some detail work to the armour, such as the gold touches, but restrain yourself from adding too much. After a slight adjustment in the Colour Balance palette (see page 119), increase the contrast slightly more.

HELMET

This step-by-step will go through the process of creating a helmet starting from traditional methods and polishing the result digitally.

Step 1: Begin by loosely sketching in the basic idea for the helmet, using a mechanical pencil with HB graphite. Even though you are concentrating on the helmet, draw a head which the helmet can rest on. This gives a better idea of the placement of a helmet on a human head.

Step 2: Switch to a softer grade graphite and use a regular B pencil to begin shading in the various areas of the helmet. Don't be overly concerned with the rendering, since you plan to paint directly over it. This is just a guide.

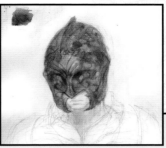

Step 3: Prepare the surface by applying a thin coat of PVA over the drawing. It dries very fast, so you can begin painting immediately. Using heavily diluted acrylic, make a mixture of Managanese blue, Pthalo and Raw umber. I used a large #12 flat synthetic brush to quickly tone the entire helmet. Because of the organic nature of using acrylic, there will be variation of colour and texture within the wash. These irregularities can really give a more natural and unique look.

Step 4: Acrylic paint dries very quickly, so I am able to work right on top of the pre-existing layer in a matter of minutes. Using small size brushes, begin adding a few more details, and start painting in the shadows.

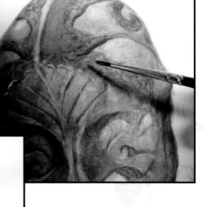

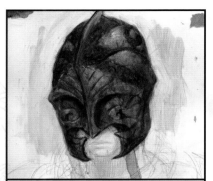

Step 5: With the basic shadows in place, add some acrylic Titanium white and start painting in the lighter values. Use swatches of colour as notation of the hues and values used. If there is a colour harmony you like, you can go back and use this to see how it was mixed. It also helps to make sure you do not stray far from the palette.

Step 6: Add some texture and roughness. Drip some thinned out acrylic over the helmet and add some loose brushwork around it. To finish in Photoshop you will need to scan it in. I recommend scanning at 300dpi at least. Open the scan in Photoshop and go to Image>Adjustments>Levels and make the necessary adjustment to the scanned image.

Step 7: Add an Overlay layer and begin adding a yellow tint to the top. Paint in blues where it does not catch the light. If you were to do this step with paint, mix a yellowish green hue and a bluish green hue. Dilute the paint, but not as thin as watercolour. Making sure the previous layer of paint is dry, apply the warm hues with a medium-sized brush.

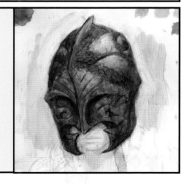

Step 8: Time to clean up the image. Use a Hard Round Brush, and with white, begin painting the areas you do not want, being mindful of the outer edges. Erase eyeholes in the helmet. To clean up the image using paint, use an opaque white and a flat synthetic brush. Use a smaller brush for the eye sockets. Paint carefully and slowly, dragging the brush to get a clean edge.

Step 9: To break up the green of the helmet, on a Colour layer use a brown to give an aged golden look with green undertones. To do this step with paint, follow Step 7, but make a mixture of yellow ochre and raw umber. Thinly paint in the areas for a brownish hue.

Step 10: Adjust the Levels (see page 119) to get greater contrast and value range. After a few minor tweaks the helmet is done!

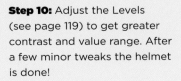

SWORD

Weapon design can be tricky. We want the weapon to look interesting and unique, but it still has to appear functional. In this step-by-step I will share my technique of using a simple silhouette and transforming it into a full colour painting of a sword.

Step 1: You just want a flat black shape to start with, so use a Hard Round Brush. Play with a few shapes and remove some black areas with a Hard Round Eraser to give the shape more interest.

Step 2: Although the sword shape is interesting, I am not satisfied with it and want a weapon that could belong to a person of higher rank or importance. I make a copy of the shape and then flip it by going to Edit>Transform>Flip Vertically. Then I line up the copy and original shape to create a new symmetrical shape when combined. The shape is really up to you, so be experimental with your choice.

Step 3: When you are happy with your basic shape, go back to refining the shape – add flat black in some areas, and carve away other areas with an Eraser. Here, I like the bulk of the sword, and really think the openings in the blade make it appear as if it would still be light enough to swing despite its size. Some of the results are unexpected, such as the top portion of the blade. It is okay not to know where you're going at this point.

Step 4: I know I want there to be a fair amount of ornamentation on this weapon, so I start making marks in grey with the Hard Round Brush. I am just following the pre-existing forms I made of the sword and mimicking them with new marks.

Step 5: It is now time to turn this flat object into something more dimensional. Lightly paint in some values on top of the shape while using consistent lighting from the top.

Step 6: With the values in place, create a new Overlay layer and use a Soft Round Brush to start applying colour to the weapon. Add another Overlay layer and add a scratchy, metallic texture on top.

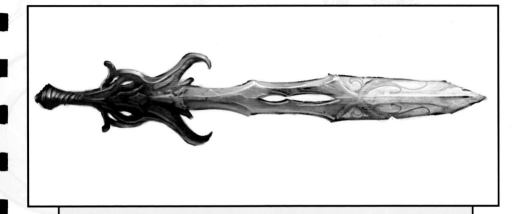

Step 7: Begin cleaning up the edges and getting rid of most of the black lines showing through. The black lines will flatten out the object, so I remove them almost completely. Begin working close up and add in the highlights and details, keeping in mind the reflective surface quality of the metal. Adding little nicks and scratches can give quite a bit more character and a realistic feeling to your weapon designs. Use a tiny Brush. Select colours and values that are close to the blade of the sword, but only slightly darker and lighter. You do not want the scratches to stand out too much. Make small marks with the tiny Brush of varying length, shape and value – some darker, some lighter.

MAGIC WEAPON

The great thing about weapons in fantasy art is that they can be just as supernatural and magical as the characters that possess them. This step-by-step will focus on creating the magic special effects of a fantasy weapon.

Step 1: Using the techniques that were covered in creating the 'Sword' project, take the silhouetted shape and flip it vertically to create a symmetrical shape. You could create something that looks fairly inert without the magic.

Step 2: Use a range of greys to give the weapon a bit more form. I keep the material of the weapon fairly dark, because I know when I paint the magical effects, things will get much lighter and I want the structure of the weapon to remain visible.

Step 3: Begin to add a bit of colour to the weapon using a Soft Round Brush on an Overlay layer. Keep the colours fairly subdued, so when you paint the magical effects, the intense colour will stand out more.

Step 4: Create a Multiply layer and start adding pink and purple hues to where you want the magic to appear. My broad idea was to have the magic appear in all the openings in the weapon structure, as if it is being generated inside somehow.

Step 5: Painting magical effects can be done in a variety of ways. For this weapon, I was thinking it would be like if you could bottle lightning. Start adding colour around the main area where the magic will occur in the weapon. To create the pink areas around the outside of the weapon continue painting on the same Multiply layer in Step 4. Using a Small Round Brush paint the splashes around the weapon.

Step 6: After adding a bit more colour to the magic effects inside the weapon, take a Hard Round Eraser and reduce the size to just a few pixels. Start making tiny scratch marks to simulate electricity flowing.

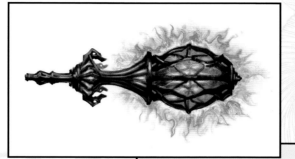

Step 7: Go to the Filter tab, and select Liquify. In the Liquify menu, start distorting the magical effects and moulding them so they almost resemble flames.

Step 8: On a new layer, drop a texture on a Vivid layer, and repeat the process on an Overlay layer (see page 80). Erase some areas on each layer, letting small areas show through to get the desired effect.

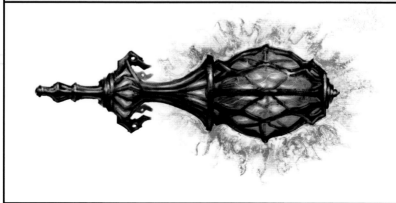

PROJECTS
CREATURE SHOP

From soaring dragons to scuttling beetles, this chapter presents you with a taster course of fantastical creature projects you could get started on, as well as the techniques to make them believable. Added tips about using Photoshop help you to give your pieces a professional finish.

ANIMAL HYBRID CREATURE

In this digital step-by-step a new creature is created by borrowing and combining elements from mainly a chimpanzee and a red panda. The result from doing this can be very effective as the creatures are both foreign, yet familiar in appearance.

Step 1: Fill the entire canvas using the Paint Bucket tool. Select a neutral, middle-value colour, as this will usually make it easier to create dimension. Very roughly sketch in the idea using a Hard Round Brush.

Step 2: You need to start to get an idea of the form of this creature, so block in big blocks of light and shadow. Break down the underlying structure of the chimpanzee's facial features. Using a Large Round Brush, begin blocking in the general light and dark. The toned background comes in useful here, as it is easy to select a a variety of values. If you are using references watch out for large areas where light and shade divide. You will need a competent knowledge of form to do this convincingly without references.

Step 3: Still working monochromatically, begin to define the forms more with most of the attention on the facial features of this creature. Start to differentiate the areas that have long fur, and the areas that are hairless. To do this, working on the same layer, continue defining values as it describes in Step 2, although reduce your Brush size and start becoming more specific.

Step 4: Start adding Overlay layers and painting colour onto the creature. The fur areas and skin colours will not only be different in texture, but in colour as well. Use orange hues for the fur, and a purplish-grey hue for the skin areas. Because orange and purple are complementary colours, they create a nice contrast and visual effect on the creature.

Step 5: Going back into the face, add more cool, purplish lights. This gives more form and interest to the face, but also creates more contrast between the orange and purple hues.

Step 6: After defining the form a bit more, take a better look at your reference of the red panda. You don't want to copy – only to get ideas on some of its physical traits. On a separate layer begin painting in light and dark markings on the fur, much like that of the red panda.

Step 7: Create a new layer called Soft Light, and drop in a fur-like texture into the layer. Set the Opacity at 45%. Erase any of the fur texture on the hairless areas of the creature.

Step 8: The overall appearance is a little more muted than I had intended, so you could try a new Adjustment layer and select Hue/Saturation. Increase the Saturation by six increments.

Being creative with texture

On a last-minute whim, you could decide it might be interesting to overlay an existing painting (see page 80). Here I overlay an old image of mine on top of this image. I go through my library of images and select a very brushy painting and put it on an Overlay layer. I reduce the Opacity until I get the desired result.

DRAGON

One of the most beloved and well-known fantasy creatures is the dragon. In this step-by-step I will cover how using creative viewpoints and composition can add another dimension to your creature designs.

Step 1: Instead of a traditional dragon, use composition and perspective to make the image more compelling. This version makes it seem as if the dragon is flying above our heads. The colours and lighting should be natural, as if it is a summer's day. Using a Large Round Brush, lay in the big shapes.

Step 2: Adjust the position of the dragon's wings so they give a more sweeping, circular motion to the image. Maintaining the idea of peering up at the dragon, bring the tail down to force the perspective a bit more. This way your eye will go up the dragon's tail and lead to his head, which is also framed by the wings.

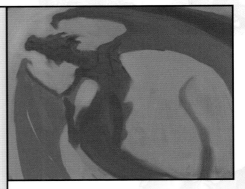

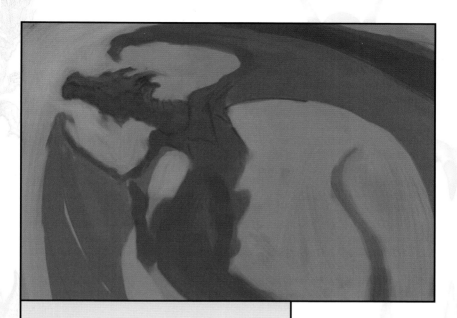

Step 3: Using a Hard Round Brush, begin to sculpt the dragon's form by adding in some lighter values. Use a warm, yellowish colour for the light parts to create some contrast with the overall cool blue hues of the image. The wings are slightly transparent and thin compared to the rest of the dragon, and light would pass through them. I show this by not only lightening them, but also adding warm, orange and reddish hues.

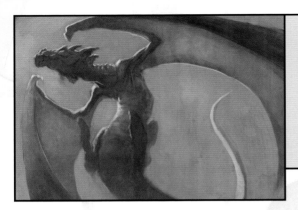

Step 4: Take a greenish-blue watercolour textured paper and set it on an Overlay layer to break up the texture of the piece.

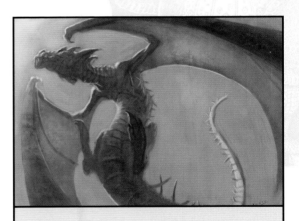

Step 5: With a Small Round Brush, go back into the dragon and start adding details. Add spiky formations to the back and tail, keeping in mind how they will react to light in their positions.

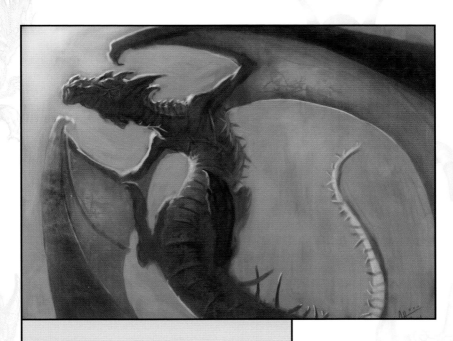

Step 6: Select Levels from the Adjustments and begin to tweak the different parameters (see page 119). Only move the black, grey and white sliders a small amount, because just a fraction makes a huge difference.

INSECT-BASED CREATURE

I wanted to create a creature that appeared to be insect-based, yet slightly alien. Instead of doing several thumbnails and sketches, try starting immediately by painting digitally, developing the idea as you go along.

Step 1: I start using a simple Round Brush and just using black. I make several marks and try to use each previous mark as a guide to the next one. I work very quickly without second guessing. The goal is to just try and create an abstract that is interesting.

Step 2: Within this abstract shape try to see recognisable shapes. Start adjusting the shape and defining its outer edges so that it starts to look more like a creature. Use the Hard Round Brush to paint in areas and use a Hard Round Eraser to remove any unwanted areas.

Step 3: Still using just a Round Brush, start defining the form by adding grey tones and further defining the anatomy of the creature. At this stage I have a clear vision of what I want my creature to look like.

Step 4: Continue to define the form, and using a small Hard Round brush, pop in a small highlight. I want this creature to appear very dark in hue, so do not want to flood it with too much light. Take a chance with the 'tail' of the creature. The rear tendrils stray a bit from the creature design, but they do give it an alien appearance.

Step 5: At this stage, include texture and some colour variation. I can achieve both of these goals by using one of my watercolour texture papers in my texture library. I paste the texture on an Overlay layer (see page 80). I do not want a lot of colour or texture, so I reduce the Opacity of the Overlay layer to approximately 25%.

Step 6: On a separate layer, include some cast shadows using a Soft Round Brush. I still want the shadows softer so I go to Filters> Blur>Gaussian Blur and set the blur radius to 4.4. Go back in with the Hard Round Brush and develop the light and shade. Add a reflected light to the head of the creature, so it appears to be more 3D.

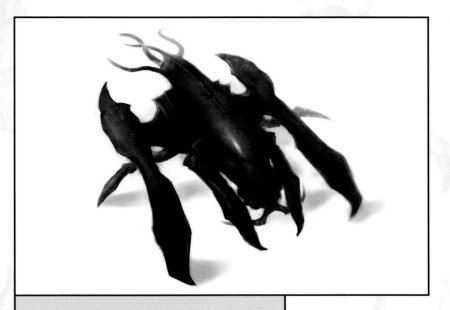

Step 7: I felt the creature's hue should remain black, but have warmer undertones, so I create an Adjustment layer and select Colour Balance. Add a bit more yellow into the Midtones (see page 119). Lastly, to sharpen some things up, make a duplicate of the entire image and paste it on top of the already existing image. Under Filters, go to Sharpen>Unsharp Mask and set the amount at about 115%. On the duplicated layer, reduce the Opacity of the image to 50%, and erase any parts you do not want sharpened. This way, the existing image on the layer underneath will show through.

ORC PRINCE

Using traditional watercolour washes as an abstract base, extract the orc head from the established textures and colours using digital painting techniques. Combining the digital with abstract traditional media like this gives a lively and visually interesting final image.

Step 1: After scanning in the watercolour wash, play around with the paper to get unusual and unexpected results. In this image, start by copying the entire image by using Select>All, then Edit>Copy> Paste. Then go to Edit> Transform>Flip Horizontal. Put the flipped image on an Overlay layer in the layers palette and adjust the Opacity to get the desired result.

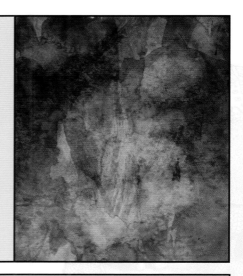

To Photoshop or not to Photoshop?

Most projects in this book could work with both traditional and digital techniques. Aside from layer and level techniques utilised in digital work, the approach is almost identical. The key is to practise the fundamentals and then they can be applied to any medium.

If you were to create this project with traditional tools, acrylic would work well over the watercolour layer. You could start drawing on top of the watercolour layer with an HB or softer pencil for the loose drawing. When you begin painting, you will want to start with thinned out acrylic (using water to dilute the paint) and begin with larger brushes. As the painting progresses use more opaque paint and begin to use smaller brushes.

Step 2: Using a Hard Round Brush do a very loose drawing and start pulling shapes from the abstract background. Use the background to get colour scheme ideas, and start including colour even though the structural drawing is still incomplete.

Step 3: Still using the Round Brush, start refining the drawing and structure. You may, like me, think that the background is overwhelming and use the Smudge tool (page 16) to soften it. My brush sizes are still large, and I am just thinking of big shapes and restraining from including details at this point.

Step 4: At this stage establish the lights and darks a bit more. Start adding and refining the features on the Orc's face. Look for areas on the face that would be affected by the light source that have not been rendered yet. The face is a complicated form, so you will need to spend a bit more time distinguishing where light and shade meet on the face of the Orc. Establishing form will also establish light and shade, and vice versa.

Step 5: Add some texture to the metal crown, dropping a texture you already have on a new layer. Set the layer to Pin Light (see page 81), and erase all the areas that you do not want texture.

Step 6: Refine some areas, and add some small details to the crown and face. Make an Adjustment layer and use the Colour Balance. Reduce the yellow in the Midtones a small amount (see page 119).

Step 7: The overall values in the painting appear slightly too uniform, so you will want to make a new Overlay layer, and with a Soft Round Brush and a light yellowish colour, lighten up directly behind the Orc's head and towards the right side of the painting to give the image more visual punch.

PROJECTS
FANTASY ENVIRONMENTS

Sinister, cheerful, peaceful, erratic – just some of the moods a good setting can deliver to a piece, even before you have included any characters. Have you ever wanted to create a floating path, or a village built into the heart of a forest? This chapter on landscapes and environments shows you how.

CASTLE ENVIRONMENT

This step-by-step will go through the stages of creating a fantasy environment from the thumbnail stage to the final digital painting.

Step 1: Start off this environment by doing several thumbnails. I usually do these in my sketchbook and try to establish the ideas quickly. I select the top left one, and decide I want to take it further.

Step 2: To get started, copy the thumbnail and paste it in a new file in Photoshop. Because thumbnails are small, increase the scale by a good amount. Even though it is just a thumbnail, it can be enough information to get started.

Step 3: Using the enlarged thumbnail as a guide, I start clarifying the values using a Large Round Brush. I start defining the shapes a little bit more as I get a better idea of where I want to take the painting.

Step 4: Still working in greyscale, develop the light and shadow more, and refine the shapes of all the elements. Your prime objective is to achieve a strong value foundation. To establish the light and shade, you will need to start making clear choices essential for representational painting. I decide the light will be coming from the right side of the painting, and will be more of a diffused, softer light as opposed to a sunny day with strong crisp light and hard-edged shadows. This will cause the objects facing the light to be in light on the right side, and in shadow on the left side.

Step 5: Create a new Multiply layer and paste a watercolour texture paper on it. This gives you a good base to start the colour portion of the painting.

Step 6: You may feel that it looks sparse and desolate. Start adding snow to further give the appearance that this castle is in a very isolated place. Create a new layer set on Normal mode. Using a Medium Round Brush, begin selecting hues that are close to white, but still have a bit of colour. Reserve using straight white for a few select spots. Start painting in snow on the rocks. Use the Eraser on areas of snow, as if it had melted and rock was peaking through.

Step 7: Add more snow and a bit more colour into the image. In the far background keep the edges soft and ambiguous to keep the focus on the foreground and the castle.

Step 8: Add additional details to the castle and make any necessary final tweaks. I suggest adding a brick texture using a Small Round Brush and more detail to the scaffolding of the castle. Clean up any edges that should have a hard and crisp edge, by using a Small Round Brush and firmly applying paint. Adjust the Colour Balance to reduce the amount of cyan in the image (see page 119). Reduce the Opacity on the Colour Balance layer by 30% and complete the picture.

FLOATING PATH

Combining traditional oil-painting techniques with digital enhancements, this step-by-step will go through the process of creating a fantasy environment with unnatural elements. This project could be completed at Step 9, before the painting is scanned into Photoshop. This depends on personal preference and how polished you wish the final piece to be.

Step 1: Looking at my thumbnails, I find the path made up of floating rock formations has potential. I like starting with Rose Col-Erase pencils because they are easy to draw with and they go on very light and it is easy to draw over them with a regular graphite pencil. With my Rose Col-Erase pencil, I make a quick two-point perspective grid. Using the grid as a guide I use a combination of my mechanical pencil with HB graphite and a 2B pencil.

Step 2: On a Multiply layer, add a purple tone to the image. Then make a large print on 250 gsm paper. Mount the print on illustration board and seal the surface so it can be painted over.

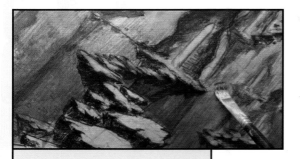

Step 3: Using a large, flat sable brush, very thinly start applying a mixture of Cadmium orange, Burnt umber and a small amount of Cobalt blue.

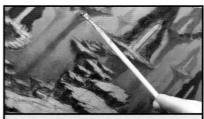

Step 4: Switch to a medium-size flat brush, and mix Titanium white, Cerulean blue and a small amount of Quinacridone red. Working thinly, paint in the regions of the rocks and background.

Step 5: Load up your palette knife with paint, and start applying it to the light areas of the rock path. This adds a good deal of texture and variation in the brushwork. The paint in the light areas should be a little thicker as the painting progresses.

Step 6: Once that layer of paint dries, use a thinned out mixture of Burnt umber and Alizarin crimson and start to apply it over the entire painting with a large flat brush.

Step 7: Working while the paint is still wet, take a clean bristle brush, and slightly dip the tip in the turpenoid. Then wipe off the excess turpenoid on a clean rag. Bring back some layers beneath by taking the bristle brush and rubbing away that section. This allows the previous layer to show through. Use a rag to wipe out larger sections.

Step 8: At this stage, start applying thicker paint. In the areas where you want the light to be really bright, load up the palette knife with a mixture of Titanium white, Cadmium orange and a bit of Cadmium yellow light. Use a small palette knife to get the thick paint into smaller areas.

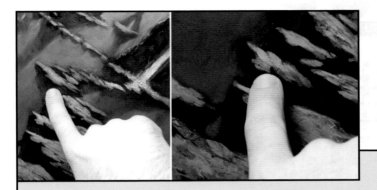

Step 9: For a subtle blurring effect on some sections, push the paint around with your finger. Do this at the late stages of the painting process. Be sure not to stick your hands in your mouth or eat anything without thoroughly cleaning your hands, as oil paints are toxic.

Step 10: When the painting is dry, transfer the image onto your computer. Sometimes I will take a photo, but if it is small enough, scan it and stitch it together in Photoshop. To do this, go to File>Automate> Photomerge. Select all the scanned sections of the painting, and Photoshop will accurately merge the scans. You may have to adjust some things, but this feature works surprisingly well.

Step 11: Some Level adjustments are usually required to match the original colours and values of the painting (see page 119). Then start with Overlay layers and a Soft Round Brush to push colours. To do this, you need to select colours that are intense. When you paint in the select areas with these intense colours, it will give the hues on the previous layer more visual punch.

Step 12: Continue overlaying layers and adjusting colours. Paint some warm oranges and reds on the bottom of the painting into the floating rocks. Bring some of the background colour into the shapes in the far background to push them back more. To do this, add a new Overlay layer, paint on it and then create another Overlay layer. Through using a few Overlay layers, subtle or drastic effects can be achieved.

Step 13: Make a duplicate of the entire image and past it on top of the original. Then go to Filter>Blur>Gaussian Blur and set the amount to approximately 7.5. Reduce the Opacity on the layer to about 60%. Erase the areas in the foreground that you do not want blurred at all.

Acrylic painting?

You could replicate these effects by mixing a thinned out red-orange hue and using a soft, synthetic, medium-sized brush and lightly applying it over the desired areas. You could not replicate a digital filter like Gaussian Blur traditionally, but you could continue to Steps 14 and 16 and paint in other small rocks traditionally with a small round detail brush.

Step 14: With a Small Round Brush start adding in other little floating rocks using the Colour Picker tool to grab colours already existing in the image.

Step 15: I add an Overlay watercolour texture and set the Opacity to only 16%. Look for subtle shifts in colour and texture, so the Overlay is not too dominant.

Step 16: The harsh darks of the rocks along the path could be competing too much with the dark shadows in the foreground. Add some more of the red hue, reflecting up from the bottom of the image. Also, add some more floating rocks in front of the largest rock formation.

Step 17: In this detailed image you can see how I lay the digital paint on top of the traditional oils. The marks I make can also be quite abstract, as I am more interested in suggestion than rendering every little pebble.

FOREST VILLAGE

My aim was to create an environment that would be more appealing to young kids and have a fairy-tale atmosphere. The approach to this environment is different in that thumbnails or preliminary drawings are not necessary.

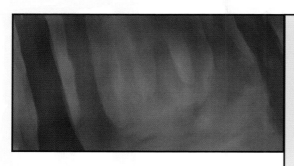

Step 1: Without any preparatory work, begin laying in large shapes which form a forest, with a Large Round Brush. The size of the trees should get smaller as they recede into the background, and they also appear much lighter.

Step 2: Start to define the sky peeking through the trees a bit more using a muted greenish-blue colour. With just a loose concept in mind I start painting in little houses attached to the trees. Because you are developing the idea while simultaneously painting, focus on one area. This can serve as an anchor point and allows you to develop the rest of the image based on that area.

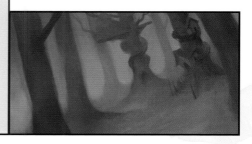

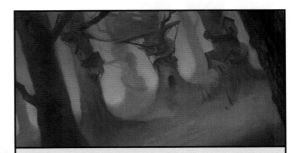

Step 3: Continue adding more huts and shacks in the forest village. Avoid adding colour to the villages in the background trees, and keep the contrast low.

Step 4: At this stage you are just about to complete the general structure of the village. Add a few details, but keep the image whimsical and not too busy with detail.

Step 5: The overall blue hue gives me the idea to try an evening scene. Create a new Multiply layer and use the Paint Bucket tool to fill the entire image with a bluish-green tint. This gives the image a uniform appearance.

Step 6: Add some warm lights emerging from the trees and huts by using a Small Round Brush and selecting colours in the orange–yellow range. Without even seeing any figures, we recognise that life must be stirring inside.

Step 7: On an Overlay layer, select a light warm orange colour and paint over the areas with warm light. This gives the light a little added glow. Paint some light hitting nearby objects that are close to the light source.

Step 8: Finish off the piece by adjusting the Levels a bit for a little contrast boost (see page 119). Move the grey middle slider slightly towards the right. Move the white slider on the left end slightly towards the middle. You will see a significant increase in contrast. Use the Blur tool (see page 16) on the elements in the far background.

RUINS ENVIRONMENT

I wanted to create a moody environment set among old ruins in a dimly lit forest. Using digital painting techniques, this step-by-step will focus on light and mood.

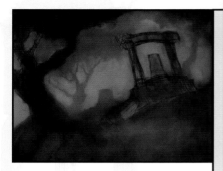

Step 1: This is another project which can start in a flexible way, so begin painting in Photoshop in a rough and abstract fashion, and do not over-commit to anything just yet. Use only large brushes and only concern yourself with shapes. You do not need to worry about well-defined edges, correct value or colour at this point. Look for an interesting arrangement of shapes.

Step 2: Start to mould the large shapes of the composition more. The area to the bottom right drew my attention. Using the rocks and grass patterns, the area turned out to actually lead the eye to the focal point.

Step 3: Using fairly large brushes, work the entire picture, giving attention to all areas and not honing in on one area at this point. Jumping around the entire image, work on several areas simultaneously. Spend a little more time at the focal point, and start suggesting the texture and surface of the ruins.

Step 4: At this point, polish off the far background elements so you can concentrate more on the focal point. Add cool greens to the sky and add more dimension to the flat tree shapes.

Step 5: Create a strong light source in one area – almost a spotlight effect. To do this, create a new Overlay layer, and with a Soft Round Brush paint in a small area at the bottom of the ruins, using a light yellow hue.

Step 6: Back in a normal layer, start adding details to various areas in the painting. Work on the rough texture of the trees and rocks, and add some cracks on the ruins. Paint some foliage in front of the ruins, then create the shadow cast from it.

Step 7: In the Colour Balance menu adjust the tones a bit to get a moodier, darker feel.

Step 8: The piece needs more information to make the scene more engaging, so begin adding texture on a darker colour layer on the main ruins. Then on a normal layer add vines wrapping around the ruins.

PROJECTS
CHARACTERS
AND VILLAINS

Fantasy character archetypes are discussed in depth on pages *66-69*. This chapter presents several easy projects which show how creative you can be with your treatment of the classic elf, hobbit, villain and hero.

ELF

Create an elvish girl in a forest setting. The first part of the step-by-step will be a traditional oil painting, and the second half will be the digital enhancements. If you wanted to continue painting traditionally, you could. Just like the 'Floating Path' project (pages 177–185), you could do the majority of enhancements with the exception of computer-specific techniques.

Step 1: On a gessoed illustration board (12.5cm x 18cm), lightly sketch the drawing with an HB pencil. Spray a light coat of fixative so the pencil marks remain. Using very diluted acrylic paint, apply a light wash of Raw umber over the entire board.

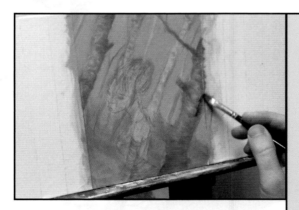

Step 2: Using a #8 flat red sable brush start thinly painting the background in big blocks. For the sky I am using a mixture of Cerulean blue and Naples yellow light. Use quite a bit of turpenoid to thin the oil paints.

Step 3: Start to thinly paint in tones on the figure using mixtures of Raw umber, Venetian red and a bit of Ivory black. Then start to decrease the size of your brushes as you start working on smaller areas. At this stage I mainly use a #4 mongoose hair bright brush.

Step 4: Flesh colours for this elf girl vary. For the light areas use a mixture of Quinacridone red, Yellow ochre and Titanium white. In the shadows, it is better to achieve a cooler hue, so use Quinacridone red, Raw umber and a cool grey mixture made from Ivory black and Titanium white. Begin adding details and smaller shapes with a size #0 red sable round watercolour brush.

Step 5: At this stage, start adding the lightest lights and dark accents using mostly small round and bright brushes. You may want to keep a lot of the roughness of the brushstrokes, so it shows through when you begin the digital portion of the image. The image is small enough to scan in when it is completely dry.

Step 6: After scanning in the image, create a new Multiply layer, and with the Paint Bucket, fill the entire image with a bluish hue.

Step 7: Now you can start painting digitally on top of the original oil painting. Use the original underneath much like an under-painting as you refine certain areas, and leave others in their original rough state. This creates a nice variety of textures and both digital and organic nuances. Clean up some edges around the perimeter of the figure and other objects in the foreground such as the tree and leaves.

Step 8: Make a new Overlay layer, and choose a light pink hue. Using a Soft Round Brush paint in areas where you want the light to be more intense. Contrasting warm colours in the light work nicely with the cool background.

Step 9: You may decide the framing of the character lends itself to a photographic depth of field. Copy the entire image and paste it on top of the original. Under Filters>Blur>Gaussian Blur I set the amount to 7.5. With a Soft Round Eraser, erase all the areas you do not want blurry. The unaffected layer underneath will show through, causing the blurry sections to recede.

HOBBIT-LIKE CHARACTER

Some of the beacons of twentieth-century fantasy literature were J. R. R. Tolkien's *Lord of the Rings* and *The Hobbit* books. In this step-by-step we will take a look at how to develop your own interpretation of a hobbit character.

Step 1: Loosely sketch some basic shapes for the hobbit. If working on paper, use HB or softer pencils. Hobbits are short, with big feet, and softer, rounder shapes depict them more accurately. Draw just enough information so that you can use this 'skeleton' as a guide, which will help you stay accurate to the description.

Step 2: With the underlying structure in place, you can now start fleshing out the features. Still working very loosely, I find it helps to draw the basic forms of the body first, and then draw the clothes after the figure has been established. When you then draw the clothing, it is easier to make it appear as if it is resting and wrapping around the body.

Step 3: This is all the information needed before you start painting. To get started, add a Multiply layer and use the Paint Bucket tool to fill the layer with a middle value tone. If you are working with traditional materials, begin working with acrylic or oil paints.

Step 4: In Photoshop, using a Round Brush, roughly paint in large areas of colour. If using acrylic or oil paint, work with the paint thinly and use a small brush. Keep the palette fairly muted at this point, so you can reserve the more intense colours for the later stages of painting. Before I finish this stage, I try to establish the basic shadow shapes.

Step 5: At this stage, refine the facial features, as they will be the focal point. Pay close attention to the skin tones, and give him a bit of a 'ruddy' look. This is emphasised more by the neutral area where his beard would be. You could, as I have, decide to vignette the piece and start erasing parts of the background.

Step 6: At this stage, start to add details and concentrate on the eyes. You could also start adding more saturated colours in the light sections of the face and red tunic.

Step 7: Drop in a watercolour wash texture on an Overlay layer to give some texture and a more organic feel to the digital painting.

Step 8: To finalise the painting, open an Adjustment layer and select Levels. Adjust the black, grey and white sliders just a little bit to finish up the piece (see page 119).

INFERNO VILLAIN

This step-by-step will take you through the process of creating a villain starting from a pencil drawing and ending with a digital painting. I wanted this villain to have flame ability, so the instructions will focus on creating the special effects of fire.

Step 1: Start drawing the basic construction of the figure with a Rose Col-Erase pencil. Concentrate on establishing a strong pose and solid anatomy.

Step 2: With a mechanical pencil, add clothing on top of the underlying drawing. Establish the larger shadow shapes and indicate where the flames will be. Once you have completed your drawing scan in your image.

Step 3: Using the Gradient tool, create a gradient that ranges from blue to brown. Set it on a Multiply layer so the underlying pencil drawing shows up clearly.

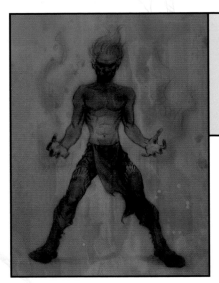

Step 4: With a Soft Round Brush, add some colour on a Multiply layer. Drop in a texture paper on an Overlay layer (see pages 80–81) to break up the flat colour.

Step 5: On a new Normal layer start rendering the image. Brushstrokes go in the direction of the forms, especially around muscles. Add a pinkish-orange hue for the flames by using a Soft Round Brush at a medium-small size. Start drawing in the fire markings on the villain.

Step 6: Using a combination of Overlay and Colour Dodge layers, paint in the highlights of the flames. Repeat the process for the flame markings on the villain by reducing the brush size and choosing a range of colours from purple to yellow.

Step 7: Adjust the Levels and Colour Balance to achieve greater contrast and push the value range (see page 119). After setting a watercolour texture on an Overlay layer (see page 80), I still felt the image needed additional work.

Step 8: Add a bit of rim light from the flames on the shoulders and upper legs. Using the Blur tool, (see page 16) blur areas around the flames and the background.

WINGED HERO

This step-by-step will go through the process of taking a scanned drawing and creating a greyscale digital painting from it. From there, you will then take the greyscale and turn it into a full-colour digital painting.

Step 1: Using a Rose Col-Erase pencil, draw the character. The armour looks ornate and somewhat regal. Playing around with proportions produces a character that has a stockier appearance than one would normally associate with a hero.

Step 2: Switching to a Blue Col-Erase pencil, develop the armour more and add the wings.

Step 3: Scan in your drawing. In Photoshop, prepare the greyscale painting. I paint a middle value grey tone on a Multiply layer over the entire figure.

Step 4: With a Round Brush, start adding the large light and shadow values. I only use shades of grey, which allows me to concentrate solely on developing the value structure and form.

Step 5: Now using a smaller Round Brush, start to develop the details. Add sharp highlights to the metal armour and render the engraved ornamentation. Adjust the face to look more attractive and less gruff. You can do this by giving him a fuller top lip. The left side of his face (the shadow side) is also very angular, so fill out his face there using a Round Brush.

Step 6: In the layer palette, create a new Colour layer. Using a Soft Round Brush choose warm, light colours and add a bit of purple in the centre for additional visual interest. Set the Opacity of the layer at 60% to use the greyscale under-painting in the metal armour.

Step 7: Complete the details and go back to rendering the face. Add warm colour to the nose to bring it forwards and give the face a bit more life.

Step 8: After a few Level and Colour Balance adjustments (see page 119) you may decide that proportions need to be adjusted too. To make the character seem more heroic, make a copy of the entire image. Using the Lasso tool (see page 14) select the head and go to Edit>Transform> Scale. Reduce the head to about 5%.

Glossary

abstraction: A technique of starting a composition process, focusing on simple shapes, tones and textures. This technique may lead on to a representational approach or continue in the abstract vein.

accent: The absolute darkest part of the shadow.

adjustment layers (Photoshop): These work in the same way as transparencies, so you can apply an adjustment (such as hue/saturation changes) on a layer and it will become an adjustment layer. You can create a stack of layers. When you look through the adjustment layer everything seen through it seems to have that adjustment. However, it doesn't actually change the layers below therefore gives you a lot of control over what you do.

archetypes: Traditional and popular aspects of an artistic genre. See page 66 for archetypes of fantasy art.

backlighting: The subject is lit from the back. This causes the subject to be in shadow, so a secondary light source is sometimes needed.

blur tool (Photoshop): This blurs the area where you paint in Photoshop.

bristol paper: A special double-surfaced heavyweight paper used for technical drawing and illustration.

cast shadow: This is the shadow cast on the surrounding surfaces from the object.

colour wash: Colouring that uses only the slightest amount of ink, applied with a wet brush.

composition: The placement or arrangement of visual elements or ingredients in a work of art, as distinct from the subject of a work.

complementary colours: Opposite colours that intensify each other when used together.

dodge and burn tools (Photoshop): The terms 'dodge' and 'burn' refer to Photoshop digital tools that are used to either lighten (dodge) or darken (burn) specific areas of a work. They are often used to either lighten underexposed areas of a photo or darken overexposed areas.

dual lighting: A subject is lit by two light sources.

en plein air: A French term for 'in the open air' – in this context painting outdoors, on location.

exaggeration: A representation of characters or environments beyond natural life, in expression, beauty, power and vigour.

foreshortening: A term used in perspective drawing to suggest that something appears closer to the viewer than it actually is, because of the angle at which it has been drawn.

half-tone: This is the transitional area from the shade into the light. The more gradual the turn of the form, the more half-tone there is. An object with a sharp edge in light and shade – like a box – will have little or no half-tone.

highlight: The brightest part in the light.

horizon: Where the land (or sea) and sky meet. A term used in perspective. The horizon may be obscured by trees or buildings, but it's important to know where it is if you're painting a realistic scene as you need to get it straight. Otherwise your painting will look as if it's falling to one side.

hyper reality: The reimaging of a world with surreal/abstract additions or a warped sense of reality.

lasso tool (Photoshop): The Lasso tools are provided in three variations. The Lasso tool and Polygonal Lasso tool which allow you to draw both freehand and straight edge selections, whilst the Magnetic Lasso is ideal for edges set against high contrast backgrounds.

linseed oil: A common carrier used in oil paint. It can also be used as a painting medium, making oil paints more fluid, transparent and glossy. It is available in varieties such as cold pressed, alkali refined, sun-bleached, sun thickened and polymerised (stand oil).

Lowbrow art: A widespread populist art movement with origins in the underground comics world, punk music, hot-rod street culture and other subcultures. It is also often known by the name Pop Surrealism.

perspective: Systems of representation in drawing and painting that create an impression of depth, solidity and spatial recession on a flat surface.

portrait lighting: The light source is overhead and off to the side. This gives a gradient light with a full range of values, which makes it clear to see the forms.

proportions: In art, the size, location or amount of one part or thing compared to another.

Masonite: A trademarked brand name of a particular type of painting board made from wood fibres and glue (resin) that is moulded into flat boards.

saturation: How much colour or ink you use on your page.

sharpen tool (Photoshop): This increases sharpness and contrast in the areas where you paint.

smudge tool (Photoshop): This blends the pixels where you paint simulating the action of dragging a finger through wet paint.

steampunk: A sub-genre of science fiction and speculative fiction, frequently featuring elements of fantasy, that came into prominence in the 1980s and early 1990s.

terminator: This is where the light and shadow meet, and is usually the darkest part of the shadow aside from the accents.

thumbnails: Smaller versions of your pages, useful for preliminary sketches of the piece and useful for organising content and action, without going into the detail of the finished pages at full size.

tone: The enhancing effect of adding grey to black and white artwork. Used to emphasise form, mood and shadow.

turpenoid: An odourless, thin, colourless medium, Turpenoid possesses the same painting properties and drying time as turpentine but is free of the strong odour that is characteristic of turpentine.

under-painting: A technique to use a very fine wash of paint as a first painting layer to plan out the composition, and add a dimensional quality to your work.

value: The lightness or darkness of a given colour.

vanishing point: In linear perspective, the point on the horizon at which receding parallel lines meet.

vignette: Any process by which there is loss in clarity towards the corners and sides of an image.

Wacom: A digital tablet used by artists for drawing on.

THE MORE YOU KNOW

Fantasy designs are everywhere, and now you've read this book you're going to be noticing them non-stop. Here are some resources that might be of interest to you and inspirational for your own fantasy–style drawing.

RECOMMENDED READING

George B. Bridgman: *Constructive Anatomy* (Dover Publications Inc., 1975)
Richard Schmid: *Alla Prima: Everything I Know About Painting* (Stove Prairie Press, 1999)
James Gurney: *Imaginative Realism: How To Paint What Doesn't Exist* (Andrews McMeel, 2009)
Mike Yamada and Felix Yoon (editors): *The Skillful Huntsman: Visual Development of a Grimm Tale at Art Center College of Design* (Design Studio Press, 2008)

RECOMMENDED WEBSITES

There is plenty of fantasy art literature to read online and every site will contain further website links.

Online versions of Andrew Loomis' excellent art and drawing books (now out of print) can be found on this site: alexhays.com/loomis
CG Hub is an online community where computer graphics artists share their latest work, tips, and tools, network with friends, search jobs and more: www.cghub.com
An accessible and creative website for digital artists can be found here: www.cgsociety.org
The website of the Gnomon Workshop provides the highest calibre training that both educates and inspires creative digital artists: www.thegnomonworkshop.com
For regular competitions where artists can submit work and be given feedback, try the CG Channel website which is also run by the Gnomon School of Visual Effects in California, USA: www.cgchannel.com

INDEX

H

half-tone 99, g215
heads
  as unit of measure 46–7
  form/structure 48–51
  monsters 64–5
  proportion adjusting 213
helmet project 138–41
heros 67
  winged hero project 210–13
highlight 99, g215
  reflection 102–3
Hobbit, The (Tolkien) 202
Hobbit-like character project 202–5
horizon lines
  action scenes 79
  perspective 112–13
hues, warm and cool 107
hyper reality 110–11, g215
  environments 117

I

ideation 28, 30–9
inferno villain project 206–10
insect-based creature project 160–5

K

kinetic factors, action scenes 78–9
Klimt, Gustav 21

L

landscapes 58–61
lasso tool (Photoshop) 14, 213, g215
layer modes, Photoshop 74, 80–1
layer palettes 17
levels adjustment
  helmet project 141
  settings 17
levels palette, Photoshop 119
libraries, research 36
light and shade 98–9
  atmospheric perspective 114
  mood 88–91, 190–3
  texture creation 72
  to add light 88

lighting 88–91
  adding 88, 169
  castle environment project 174
  definition 82–3, 86–7
  fantasy 91
  forest village project 186–9
  reference shots 96
linseed oil g215
liquify tool 149
Lord of the Rings (Tolkien) 202
Lowbrow art 23, g215

M

magic weapon project 146–9
maidens 69
Masonite g215
McCay, Winsor 27
mechanical pencils 122
medieval era settings 52
mediums 11
  oil paints 125
Metropolitan Museum of Art 36
Michelangelo, Sistine Chapel 20
mid-tone 99
modern style 19
monochromatic sketching 152–3
monsters 64–5
mood and lighting 88–91
  ruins environment 190–3
moralistic themes 52
mouth, positioning 50
movement
  action sequences 76–9
  composition 85–7
  diagonal 79, 86–7
Munch, Edvard 21
museums, research 36

N

naturalism from abstraction 38–9
noses, positioning 50

O

objects definition 82–3, 86–7
ogres 68

CREDITS

All other images are the copyright of Quintet Publishing Ltd.
While every effort has been made to credit contributors, Quintet
Publishing would like to apologise if there have been any
omissions or errors – and would be pleased to make the
appropriate corrections for future editions of the book.

T = top, L = left, C = centre, B = bottom, R = right, F = far

Alamy: 21 © The Art Gallery Collection / Alamy; 22T © Steven May /
Alamy; 22B © Pictorial Press Ltd / Alamy; 23L © Illustration Works /
Alamy; 23R © Illustration Works / Alamy; 27T © Old Paper Studios /
Alamy; 27B © North Wind Picture Archives / Alamy.
Corbis: 26 © Christie's Images / Corbis.
istock: 10BL; 42.
Shutterstock: 10BR; 20; 30; 31B; 36; 61B; 76; 96 L, C, R.